Wanted → A New Career

The Definitive Playbook for Transitioning to a New Career or Finding Your Dream Job

Marlo Lyons

Future
Forward
Publishing

Published in the United States by Future Forward Publishing, Scottsdale, AZ

ISBN 978-1-7370181-2-4 (print)
ISBN 978-1-7370181-0-0 (epub)

Interior design and production by Dovetail Publishing Services
Editing by Matthew Gilbert
Jacket design by Jeff Zwerner

Dedication

*This book is dedicated to my husband, Brett,
and my children, Macey and Brenner.*

*Thank you for all your support by giving me time
on Sunday mornings to write this book.*

Special Thanks

*To my mom and dad, Ruth and Richard Brawer,
and my sister Gynette Parker for believing in
me every time I pursued career changes.*

"It's never too late to be what you might have been."

—George Eliot, English Victorian novelist

Contents

Foreword

Wanted → *A New Career* is needed now more than ever! The headlines of 2020 about layoffs are still impacting workers and families today. Exceptionally high unemployment levels during the COVID-19 pandemic in such industries as airlines, travel, entertainment, hotel, restaurant, oil and gas, and others will forever reshape the way we look for work and pursue our careers. Being laid off or transitioning from one career to another can seem overwhelming, but this book takes away all the fear and excuses with strategic and tactical guidance to leverage experience, knowledge, and skills for each person's situation for success.

Wanted → *A New Career* caused me to pause and reflect on my own life and the changes I have made in my career journey. As Marlo writes, there are specific transferable skills and abilities that can carry you from one job to the next. How you highlight those capabilities matters. When looking back, I remember after graduating from the University of Maryland in 1972, I took a road trip across the country. En route, my van broke down while visiting Yosemite National Park. In order to pay the mechanic bill and continue on my trip, I needed to get a job. So, I applied my Boy Scout experience and my bachelor's degree in marketing to land a job at the Yosemite Mountaineering Center. Within six months, I was managing the shop, and on my days off, I climbed the park's massive walls and cross-country skied in the winter months. From there, I traveled back east to Vermont and utilized my managerial skills to run the cross-country ski shop and teach people cross-country skiing at the Trapp Family Lodge, where I would take the singer Maria von Trapp skiing every week when she was alive. Taking this knowledge and experience further, I went on to manage and teach at the Bolton Valley Ski Touring Center. I also developed the Telemark Tuesdays Ski Program where you ski on metal-edged cross-country skis down alpine slopes.

I also realized that while I never formally worked in marketing as a career, I gained valuable marketing experience as an entrepreneur with my mother when we created a natural food energy bar, *Mothers Nutters,* in the late '70s and became the official supplier to the U.S. Biathlon Team at the 1980 Winter Olympics in Lake Placid, NY. From there, I transitioned to a completely different career, landing the Assistant Director of Admissions position at Goddard College, where I made use of my presentation skills and marketing experience to increase student enrollments. I then transitioned again, to state government, drawing on my entrepreneurial, teaching, leadership, and presentation skills to develop and lead the Supervisory Training Program to train government staff for the State of Vermont.

Even as I transitioned careers and industries, I was thirsty for knowledge and continuously curious about what I didn't know. So, I went back to school for my second master's degree in Organizational Development and eventual doctorate degree in Human and Organizational Systems. There I met Michelle, fell in love on the dance floor, married, and once again drew on all of my experience to establish our practice together: *Reina Trust Building*®. For 30 years, *Reina*® has been supporting leaders and their organizations in transforming their workplace cultures based on a foundation of trust, healing, and renewal.

Each of my jobs provided me with skills that translated into knowledge and experience that substantiated my ability to tackle the next job and the next job and the next. Utilizing my varied skills in different scenarios, each position was a stepping-stone to my next position, even when I had never worked in the next career or industry. This book highlighted for me how I used those skills to achieve the goals of whatever new organization I was looking to work for while doing what I loved and furthering my career.

Wanted → A New Career can do the same for you. It doesn't matter if you are employed, underemployed, or unemployed and desperate to put food on the table and pay your bills. Every skill, ability, and experience you have can be framed though the lens of the new job or career you seek, empowering you to choose what you *WANT* to do and avoid what you *DON'T WANT* to do.

And no matter what your story is, this book will support you in pursuing a career that is right for you. Marlo's proven *Career Transition Strategies®* will appeal to those who know what they want to do but don't have experience doing it. It will be a primer for newly minted college graduates starting their first job. It will also be of interest to those who have been fired or furloughed and need a job outside of their current field. Finally, it will be valuable for those who have been out of the workforce for years and need a proven plan to re-enter the market.

Most importantly, you will find the author's open, honest account of overcoming obstacles in her own development—as a white-collar professional, a career coach, and a human being—to be raw and revealing, captivating, and compelling. She willingly shares the fears and hopes she encountered on her journey that ultimately led to a practical, step-by-step approach for how to transition careers—not out of some textbook, but a confirmed methodology that she has lived herself.

So, what are you waiting for? This is your life. Go out and create it the way you want!

Yours in trust,
Dennis
Stowe, Vermont
January 2021

Dr. Dennis S. Reina is co-author, along with Dr. Michelle Reina, of *Trust and Betrayal in the Workplace,* 3rd ed; and *Rebuilding Trust in the Workplace.*

Preface

"The straight line, a respectable optical illusion which ruins many a man."

—Victor Hugo, French poet, *Les Misérables*

Everyone has a different career journey. What you do with that journey will determine if you are in a job you love or hate. I could have never anticipated my career path when I graduated from college. When I first left to attend college, I remember my father saying goodbye and reminding me one last time, "College is a time to grow up. The goal is to graduate with a job." So, after graduating from The George Washington University, I knew I had limited time to find a job. Otherwise, I would have to move home and I did *not* want to do that. I was certain that it wouldn't take too long because I did everything I could to prepare for a career as a TV news reporter.

This was in the early '90s. I had internships on my resume that included WRC-TV (the NBC affiliate in Washington, D.C.), CNN, and CBS News Nightwatch where I worked for Lee Cowan, now a CBS News National Correspondent. I also interned for a small start-up production company, Capitol Video, interviewing up-and-coming stars like Flavor Flav, Queen Latifa, and Martin Lawrence in exchange for the videographer helping me create a reporter resume tape. Thirty resumes and videos went out the door. Not one call. I convinced my father the only way I would get a job is if I was in front of news directors. I wanted to drive from D.C. to Texas and back and interview at every TV station along the way.

At the time there were three affiliates in each market: ABC, NBC, and CBS. I planned to hit all three before leaving each city and prepared myself for three weeks of hardcore job hunting. Every interview ended the same way, either noncommittal or, more often, "You don't have any (or enough) experience." I was even rejected for low-level writer jobs. One Nashville news director said, "Look, someone told me I'd never make it to where I am today and now, well, here I am. You'll get there, just not here." Even though I knew Nashville was too big of a city to break in, I still felt hopeless.

I arrived back in D.C. with no job and no prospects. But there was a message on my answering machine! "Hi, Marlo, this is Renard Maiuri. I'm the news director at KDRV-TV and I'd like to talk to you about an associate producer role I have in Medford, Oregon." Oregon! My job would be to take prepackaged medical stories provided to TV stations nationwide, rewrite them shorter, have a local doctor record his own voice on them, and then edit the story together. It wasn't a reporting job, but I didn't care. All I knew was I got a job in my field of choice!

Since that first job, I have had eight different careers and more than a dozen jobs. I have been a TV news associate producer; a TV news reporter (including a consumer/investigative reporter) in five states; an operations attorney for an insurance company; an entertainment lawyer managing reality show diligence and production risk at NBC and Viacom; a screenwriter; a movie producer; a career and executive coach; an HR business partner; and now, career number nine: an author! All were completely different careers, though not all of them successful or full-time. Some were "dream jobs" I pursued with vigor. Some were day jobs while I pursued other dreams. I had some traction in each one and each one helped me further figure out who I was and what I wanted. That is my biggest goal for this book: That it helps you figure out who you are, what you want, and how to get it! And once you do get it, you'll learn how to employ my proven *Career Transition Strategies*® to change again throughout your career as you continue to seek personal happiness and career satisfaction. After all, life isn't linear.

Introduction

"Everything you've ever wanted is on the other side of fear."
—George Addair, humanitarian, spiritual teacher

The number one reason why people feel stuck and don't change careers or jobs is fear.[1] Fear of the unknown. Fear of the expectations of a new role. Fear of failure. Fear is debilitating and will keep you from pursuing your dream job or at least one that fulfills you. Every reason you have told yourself as to why you haven't pursued another career has a place in your fear folder.

I remember desperately wanting out of my legal career, but my husband worked for himself at the time. I carried the family healthcare insurance. I had the 401K match. I had the "long-term incentive plan" (LTIP), aka yearly stock handouts. I believed I couldn't change jobs because I had to be the stable one as his income fluctuated from month to month depending on the deals he closed. I could have changed careers, but my excuse was that "one of us needs to have a steady paycheck." Also, I needed flexibility as a mom of two young children, and my position provided a lot of flexibility. I couldn't be sure a new job would work out or that I would be happy or I would have the flexibility I needed. They all seemed like good reasons at the time.

I'm guessing you've had your own struggles with this. What excuses have you used?

→ I am stuck because I have only done one type of job.

→ I am stuck because I just can't do what I dream of.

→ I am stuck because I don't know what I would want to do.

→ I am stuck because I really don't want to work anymore but I have to, so I'd rather stay in my current job even if I don't like it.

→ I am stuck because I need the flexibility I have in my current job and I won't have that somewhere else.

→ I am stuck because I waited "too long" to make a change and now I'm over 30 (or 40 or 50 or 60).

→ I am stuck because I built up my vacation time and I'd have to start over.

→ I am stuck because I make too much money (aka "I have golden handcuffs").

→ I am stuck because I have responsibilities (student loans, kids, other obligations).

→ I am stuck because I didn't get a higher education.

→ I am stuck because I need to go back to school to do what I want to do, and I don't have the time or money to do that.

→ I am stuck because my resume isn't ready.

→ I am stuck because I'm pregnant (or just had a baby).

→ I am stuck because I don't have time to apply for jobs.

→ I am stuck because I've been unemployed for too long (a month, six months, years).

→ I am stuck because I have a criminal record from when I was younger, and it will show up on the background check for a new employer.

→ I am stuck because I have a gap in my resume when I traveled the world or took care of a parent or took time off to raise children or did nothing at all.

→ I am stuck because I was fired from my last job and I don't know how to explain that to new employers.

→ I am stuck because I do not know what else I want to do.

I have used a lot of these reasons at some point in my life to explain why I was stuck, and yet, most of all, I had no idea what I wanted to do. When my husband changed his trajectory and took a new job at a corporation, he suddenly had health insurance, a 401K, and an LTIP. In that moment, I knew I had no more excuses for not changing careers, but I was stuck, not because of all those things, but because I was paralyzed with fear. I had no idea how to even start figuring out what I wanted to do.

What if I said the only thing "sticking you" is you? If someone told me that at the time, I would have waved them off. It's not about me! But it was, so indulge me for a few minutes. Think about a time you wanted something so bad, you would have done anything to get it. Did you let fear get in your way? If the answer is "No," then why would fear keep you from pursuing a new career? What I find, though, is that most people who answer "No" allow the six inches between their ears to turn that "No" into the excuses just mentioned.

I think back to when I was hunting for my first, second, or third jobs; nothing would have stopped me. I was ambitious and believed I could make anything happen. I never thought about failure. I just kept going, kept trying, kept believing in myself. In hindsight, I probably believed too much in myself. When I was a reporter, people would often tell me I looked like Katie Couric since we had the same haircut. So when she left NBC, I applied for her job! Hysterical, right? I wasn't even an anchor—just a small-town reporter in Dayton, Ohio. But I believed I could do anything. Then I was fired.

I walked into work at WDTN-TV early one day because my boss had told he me wanted to talk about my contract, which was coming up for renewal. When I arrived and he waved me in, I saw that another lady was there as well. I had no idea she was from Human Resources. Notebook in hand, my back had stiffened, expecting a negotiation. Then the words came out of his mouth: "We are terminating your employment immediately." Stunned, I didn't hear another word after that.

Look Deep: What Has You Stuck?

I was depressed long before that day I was fired. Six months earlier, my fiancé and I broke up. His last words to me were, "You're always so angry." He was right; I was angry. Angry his parents told him only after we were engaged that they didn't accept our relationship. Angry because he wasn't man enough to stand up to them. Angry it all crumbled. It was my first true heartbreak. And so yes, I was angry and sad, but I was just 26 and didn't realize how much my emotions had trickled into my work.

My actual work never suffered, but as I vented my frustration about this or that during the following six months, my news director never asked me why I was so angry or why I wasn't wearing my engagement ring. He never gave me any warnings or the common courtesy of a discussion about my demeanor, and he certainly never encouraged me to get help. To me, the firing was just more validation that he was a jerk. After all, he was the same guy who had told Julie Chen, who sat two cubes away, that she would never be an anchor and never "make it to network." (For those who don't know, she's now the host of *Big Brother*. Ha!) I didn't expect him to be my therapist or counselor, but I did expect some conversation, some compassion, some curiosity.

There was a pretty good chance that even if he had given me some warning or had a conversation about my emotional upset—about letting frustration and anger get the best of me when things didn't go as planned—I don't believe I was self-aware enough to have heard him. The idea of emotional intelligence had not yet entered the lexicon. The second I was fired, I was so focused on him being a jerk and his action of firing me that I didn't look inside for answers, yet.

Knowing I would run out of money in six weeks, I started reaching out to everyone I knew, which wasn't too many people since I didn't understand the concept of networking or "It's who you know." I spent eight hours a day calling people and asking about reporter openings. I wasn't even sure I wanted to stay in TV news, so I started researching and calling friends in other fields as well. The most transferrable field was public relations. I read news releases daily and I was an excellent writer so I could certainly craft one. But in call after call, I was told I would have to start at the bottom making less than $15,000 a year. I just couldn't do that, so I decided to get back in the TV news business to get out of the TV news business. No matter where I landed, I would go to law school at night. I never wanted to practice law, but I knew that having the degree would mean stability and I was all about stability after the past year of everything being ripped away.

Two weeks later, one of my few contacts, Kenn Venit, told me about a freelance reporting job in Connecticut. I spoke with the news director, Paul Lewis, who was willing to bring me on immediately. It was temporary and I had to be there in three days. I was nearly out of cash and knew I had to take the risk. If it worked out and I could parlay it into a full-time job, I would have taken a huge step up from the job in Dayton.

I put all my furniture and personal belongings in storage, packed two suitcases, and drove from Dayton to Hartford to work for WTIC-TV, Fox 61. The next day I started and was told my seat was next to another reporter, Shelly Sindland. She and I clicked as if we had known each other for years. She said she had an extra room and offered to rent it to me since she spent most of her time with her boyfriend.

I would go to work, go back to the apartment, eat dinner, go to bed, and start all over again the next day. I did my job well, but I was depressed over my breakup and now my tenuous job situation and unmotivated to apply for other jobs, even though I didn't know how long this one would last. I could barely get out of bed on the weekends, and some weekends I never changed out of my pajamas.

Then, Shelly and her longtime boyfriend broke up. As someone who not too long ago had gone through the same thing, I knew I could be a good ear for her. We decided to take walks every weekend to get into shape. We talked about dreams and what we wanted out of life. We blasted Cher's "Strong Enough" to walk a little faster and raise our spirits. Neither of us felt "strong enough," but it felt good to sing out loud and even smile for a moment, even if the smile didn't last.

Three great things came out of these walks. One, I became more aware of how I contributed to my firing and other frictions I had created in previous positions. I was embarrassed by my immature behavior and thought about what I could have done differently in Dayton. I knew I wouldn't—couldn't—repeat the same mistakes again. Two, they motivated me to start applying for full-time reporter jobs. And three, Shelly and I remain friends to this day.

Two weeks before my freelance job at WTIC was to end, I interviewed at KWTV-TV, the CBS affiliate in Oklahoma City. I knew the question was going to come up: "Why did you leave WDTN and go to WTIC for a freelance role?" Shortly after leaving WDTN, the station was sold to a new conglomerate. Perfect. My answer was simple. "The station was up for sale and my contract wasn't renewed during that time, so I found a great freelance role at WTIC. But there wasn't budget to turn it into a head count, so that's why I'm interviewing here." I didn't lie; I just put two facts together even if that wasn't the real reason I left Dayton. "Backdoor references," where the station would call someone not on your list to check you out, weren't as common back then. They offered me the job and I took it. After another cross-country drive, I was now a "consumer investigative reporter." As soon as I started, I did three things:

1. I went to the library and reserved every book I could find about anger management.

2. I found a therapist to help me work through my depression.

3. I started looking into law schools and applying for fall because I wanted a solid career backup that wouldn't require a huge pay cut to start over.

I was starting to gain some self-awareness and knew I needed help; thus, the anger management books. I began by focusing on my "anger response": When something angered me, how angry did I get? What did I feel inside? Why did I get so riled up? What would the appropriate reaction be to the situation at hand? I worked on it every day. For example, whenever I called customer service for any reason and they weren't helpful, I worked on it. It was a long process with a lot of failures and recalibrations. It took more than six months for my anger to disappear. I remember calling my mother and saying, "I called customer service because the item I bought didn't work and they didn't offer any solutions and I felt nothing! Nothing! No anger, no rising temperature! Nothing! And I resolved the issue calmly!" I was learning how to let the daily distresses roll off my back. Today, most people don't believe I ever had a major anger issue (except when I ask my kids to come to the dinner table five times and they ignore me).

About halfway through my anger management training, I found a therapist to work through my depression over my ex. At the first meeting, I cried while telling the tale of the relationship and the breakup. At the end of the second meeting, she said to me, "Okay, you've told me the whole story and I understand it. But what I don't understand is why you think the breakup is all your fault?" Wow. I didn't realize I had internalized that assumption. Maybe it was because his last words to me were, "Why are you angry all the time?" With those words, my dream of two kids and a white picket fence crumbled and it was all my fault (I had been telling myself subconsciously). But the therapist's question miraculously stopped the self-blame.

The next morning, I had a bounce in my step for the first time in nearly a year. I thought it wouldn't last but it did, and just like that, I was no longer depressed, as if someone had snapped a finger. With this new buoyancy, my motivation returned and I applied to Oklahoma City University Law School. The internet was starting to emerge and people were reading the AP wire on it. It wouldn't be long before TV news would no longer be the main source of news. My timing could not have been better.

You Are in Control

Even after I successfully changed careers, I always had to overcome obstacles that could have kept me stuck or continued to paralyze me from taking control. For example, I practiced law for six years in California and was given top performance reviews. When I applied for a higher role, I was told I wouldn't get the job because "You went to the wrong law school." Say what? I graduated No. 2 in my class, passed the California bar in one try, and was considered a top performer. And yet the name of the school on my law school graduation certificate would keep me from advancing into a more prestigious role? Then I moved to HR and watched a boss put all his time and energy into growing another employee without providing me (or others) with any growth opportunities. But I wouldn't have it. I made conscious decisions to move on.

My point in all this: You are never stuck. The only thing "sticking you" is you. I've been fired. I've been angry. I've been depressed. I've been overlooked. I've hit glass ceilings. I've been in a career that went nowhere. I've been lost not knowing what to do with my life. I get it. I will never dismiss anyone's feelings or state of mind or circumstances when dealing with the challenges of job change and career transformation. But in this book, I will take away every excuse you've ever made. This book is not about rhetoric or theory. It is a practical, step-by-step guide for how to transition careers even if you don't have any obviously relevant experience.

Before you start reading this book (or during it), figure out what is causing your stuck-ness and find resources to help unstick you.

- → If you are depressed, find a therapist.

- → If you are lost or sabotaging yourself with internal negative dialogue, find a life coach.

- → If you are concerned about finances, find a way to reduce costs, pay off student loans, and/or find a financial planner or coach.

- → If you need education, find a class or free YouTube tutorials on your subject of interest.

- → If you have a medical issue, work on it with the right specialists.

Finally, own your future. Only you can decide if this is the right time to transition careers. That decision should be made based on facts and reality. Don't let fear control that decision for you. The *Career Transition Strategies®* in this book will help you understand what it takes to transition careers and how to do it when you are ready. Now let's get started . . .

Only *You* Hold You Back

"Life isn't about finding yourself. Life is about creating yourself."
—George Bernard Shaw, playwright

When you get to the office, or wherever you work or you log on for the day from home, what are you feeling? Do you love it? Do you race to work because you are excited to start the day, talk to the people you are meeting with, jump into the project you are working on? For most people, work is just that: work. It's something we do for 8–10 hours per day to pay the bills, put food on the table, and maybe take a nice vacation or two. But you would never find Bill Gates or Richard Branson or Sheryl Sandberg or Oprah Winfrey saying that. They are driven by passion. They wouldn't be working in the fields they are in if they weren't incredibly excited about what they do every day.

> *"Like my friend Warren Buffet, I feel particularly lucky to do something every day that I love to do. He calls it 'tap dancing to work.'"*
> —Bill Gates

> *"The best advice I could give anyone is to spend your time working on whatever you are passionate about in life."*
> —Richard Branson

"It is a luxury to combine passion and contribution. It's also a very clear path to happiness."

—Sheryl Sandberg

"Everybody has a calling. And your real job in life is to figure out as soon as possible what that is, who you were meant to be, and to begin to honor that in the best way possible for yourself."

—Oprah Winfrey

Yeah, they're famous and rich so of course they love their jobs. How about normal people? You know, us. Well, here are a few "regular people" who can't be so easily dismissed:

"I'm excited about the day and what new is going to happen. Who's going to call, what special project is going to walk in. When you meet with a customer who has an idea and there's land and there's nothing on it and 12 months later there's a building, that's exciting. From concept to reality."

—Craig Fishman, principal and COO, NES Group
(bank design and architecture), Massachusetts

"Having lost my sight, I am grateful every day for the technology that enables me to work for the people who have developed it and for the people with whom I interact."

—Marc Brawer,
DM Engineering, Israel

"I was a bookkeeper for twenty-plus years which was interesting but not exciting. Cooking and good food has always been our passion. Now we run B&B Applebarn Cottage, a small bed and breakfast with gourmet food and we get to meet so many interesting characters."

—Patricia Ann Spencer, B&B Applebarn Cottage,
United Kingdom

"I love being able to speak to someone who is nervous and tailor their experience by making them feel comfortable mentally, physically, and emotionally with their surgery and confident they will have a great outcome."

—Shelly Gierat, certified registered nurse
anesthetist, California

"When I was young, I never pictured myself working in any office. Starting the organic chicken shop was fulfilling and feels like a bold step into a bright future. Waking up is easier and fun because of the feeling that my business depends on my sacrifice to make it better than it was yesterday."

—Emmanuel Msudi Nueli, entrepreneur/owner:
Kuku Kalcha Organic Food House, Kenya

"I wake up with excitement. Who am I going to see today? Who am I going to talk to? What conversation am I going to have? It's a mystery and a surprise, always something different."

—Celeste Weber, hairstylist, California

Tip #1: There are no excuses for not pursuing your dream career.

There is no perfect time to make a career transition. Just ask Wendy Sterling, a divorce recovery specialist and founder/CEO of The Divorce Rehab, whom I met through her husband when I worked with him. Wendy built a successful career in advertising for nearly two decades. She worked for Radio Disney, *Entertainment Weekly*, Café Moms, Style Hall, and Refinery29. She built her reputation as someone who could start from zero and reach millions of dollars in revenue. Just as she was about to start a new job at Clique, her world fell apart.

"The week before I was starting at Clique, I discovered my husband was having an affair with a colleague." After kicking him out, she put on a brave face and pretended she was fine at work while raising her two young sons. She was actually miserable and performing at what she described as 60% of optimal. She tried working on her marriage for a while, then finally gave up and asked for a divorce, only to learn that same day that her mom was diagnosed with ovarian cancer. She was at her absolute lowest when she realized her heart was no longer in advertising. That's when she saw my Facebook post about finishing my coaching certification. She was intrigued.

"I remember thinking about how much I loved mentoring, leading, helping others be the best they can be, but I hated revenue goals and pressure from management to sell *one more thing*." She wanted to start her own business but didn't know what that business would be. A three-hour phone call changed that.

"I could tell that in some ways you were coaching me and, at the same time, just telling me what coaching was like. I knew in that instant that I would be a coach because that's what I loved to do."

She hung up the phone and immediately signed up for a coaching course. "I remember driving to the hotel for the first course and thinking, *What am I doing?* I was so scared. I was terrified of walking into that conference room. I didn't know what to expect. Could I handle it with everything going on? It wound up being the best three days of my life."

Just as she enrolled in the certification classes, she was laid off, going from a six-figure salary to nothing but alimony and a savings account. But she knew from building up other people's advertising businesses that she was an entrepreneur at heart. Now she would be tested in starting her own business, especially when friends and family weren't entirely supportive. "No one understood what a life coach was. I got a lot of blank stares and, 'That sounds great but what are you going to do for money?'" She started coaching executives in leadership positions and realized it didn't feel authentic to her, so she moved to what felt natural: Coaching people going through divorce.

Wendy didn't throw away a thriving career; she leveraged what she'd learned to start a new one. "I used my experience in ad sales and cold calling to build my business. I busted my ass to learn about the space from others in the space including other coaches, divorce attorneys—you name it—and they helped me build my credibility." She created the brand herself, launched a divorce summit and divorce rehab group course, and a podcast, "The Divorced Women's Guide." Within one year of becoming certified, she was recognized as one of the premier divorce coaches.

"The biggest lesson I learned," she said, "was trusting my intuition and believing in myself. I looked confident in other people's eyes, but I still had to believe I could do it and be successful. In starting my own business, I found myself. I've never been happier."

Her advice to others who are hesitant to make a change? "Don't wait! You can do it if you want to. You are stronger than you know."

Is It Time for a Job or Career Change?

If you are reading this book, you want to know how to find the passion that excites you every time you get up in the morning. Start by sitting at your desk and asking yourself these six questions:

1. Do I love what I do but hate my boss?

2. Do I love my job but the company or team I work for is toxic?

3. Have I become too complacent about what I do even though I can't see myself in this career for the next 20–30 years?

4. Do I hate my job (or been fired) and/or want a completely new career but have no idea what I want to do?

5. Do I know what I want to do but have no experience doing it?

6. Am I in high school or college or about to graduate and still haven't figured out what I want to do?

If you answered yes to any of the above questions, a new job or career may be the best solution. But I am going to separate #1 and #2 from the rest. If they best describe your reality, you may just need some tools to get along better with your boss or to figure out what part you may play in the problem or the solution. If you could fix either your boss or the team/

company, you may not want to leave your job or change careers. So, let's talk about the first two and get them out of the way.

1. Do I love what I do but hate my boss? I have had some really bad bosses. They ranged from passive-aggressive "right-fighters" (aka bosses who had to be right even if the facts in front of them said they were mistaken) and bosses who micromanaged to bosses who never asked questions before jumping to conclusions or never gave feedback or promoted anyone. It took me a long time to figure out how to deal with bosses whom I felt were ineffective leaders or knew how to manage up and sideways but not how to communicate or manage down. If you love your job and want to stay but hate your boss, you will have to figure out how to get along and not worry about what he or she is or isn't doing.

My entertainment jobs were the best in the world when they came up at cocktail parties, but the reality wasn't nearly as exciting. True, I was an "entertainment lawyer" in Los Angeles and the list of my responsibilities was impressively long. My last title was Vice President, Business & Legal Affairs, Labor & Employment, Production Risk Team. Fancy, huh? My team handled all of Viacom's reality show due diligence including reviewing background checks, psychological examinations, and medical exams on all participants across Viacom's numerous channels (MTV, VH1, CMT, LOGO, Nickelodeon, etc.). We also assessed TV show productions for risks such as foreign travel needs (visas, work permits, etc.), child labor compliance, immigration into the U.S., safety and security of crews and participants, and so on. Prior to Viacom, I worked in the same field at NBC but with a smaller scope. I vetted all the participants on *The Apprentice* and most of the *Real Housewives* cast on Bravo as well as *America's Got Talent* and shows like *Teen Mom* and *Real World*. The list is in the hundreds.

Soon after I started at Viacom, though, I was frustrated. Every idea I had about making the work more efficient and providing better communication was met with what felt like roadblock after roadblock. Even after I had proven myself, it felt like my boss didn't trust me. As hard as I tried, I couldn't build a relationship with her in a productive way. She was the head of the entire Labor & Employment group, the team that handled terminations and HR investigations and dealt with litigation. She told me Production Risk wasn't her expertise, that it was handed to her when she started her job about six months before I accepted mine. The more I pushed, the more she retreated. It got so bad that our weekly calls were either five minutes long or didn't happen at all. I felt I had no support from her in my day-to-day job scope. Then, at a team development meeting, she brought in a speaker who taught us about workplace Social Styles.[1] I learned I was an Expressive with some Driver. My boss was an Amiable. I listened intensely during the exercise, which had us divide into corners of the room and write about our communication style and how we communicate during conflict.

I immediately saw my boss in the opposite corner of the room. It struck me hard. I learned that Amiables are exceptional listeners and internalize others' problems. They are concerned about being well-liked and are very patient with people. They are good at building relationships but aren't usually the people who can drive a project home or get things done because they aren't task-oriented. Amiables also avoid conflict and sugarcoat tough conversations. Ding! Ding! Ding! Ding! I finally understood my boss and how to communicate with her! I also understood why she couldn't communicate directly with me and why her feedback was so soft that I had to ask others to interpret it. I immersed myself in learning everything I could about Amiables.

I had been communicating with her in all the wrong ways, reminding, asking, even begging her to do tasks I needed done to move my own work forward. That made sense to me because I was an Expressive/Driver. I liked to check off boxes and get stuff done. No wonder we didn't get along. It was like oil and water every day. It's not that she was mean. She was just communicating in a way I didn't understand. When she gave me feedback to "slow down," for example, I translated that as my boss had no clue about how much work was on my desk. In fact, she was trying to say, "It's not how many tasks you complete; it's about the bigger picture. Focus on being more strategic, not tactical." She never actually said those words, and at the time there was no way I could have come up with that, but looking back now as a much more self-aware person, it all made sense!

At the time, though, I at least internalized enough from that training session to realize I couldn't expect her to change, so I had to change *my* communication style. I had been asking her for months to approve vendor agreements that had since expired but she would never get to it. I even forwarded her the new template over and over and she never responded. Wrong move. Amiables don't like to be pushed. So, I stopped pushing and made a conscious decision that if it wasn't important to her that vendors were charging whatever they wanted and we weren't protected by an agreement, then I shouldn't care either. I had my saved emails in a file so I could prove I tried to get her attention if anyone ever questioned why we didn't have new agreements. And with that, I let it go. I stopped asking for anything and rarely raised issues so I wouldn't have to "push" for an answer. I rebuilt my "relationship" with my boss by speaking her language.

By just changing how I communicated with her with no expectation that she would change, our relationship did change. Our weeklies went from tense and short back to their scheduled 30 minutes. I joked and kept things light at the beginning of the calls instead of jumping right into work mode. Since Amiables are about relationships, I allowed time for small talk even if that took most of our one-on-one time. Though I hated small talk and usually needed approval for a project or to resolve an issue, I put my natural inclinations aside and talked about relationships I was building instead of work I was accomplishing. I didn't ask her questions but presented specific issues and gave her lots of information, so she was comfortable with the decisions I was making. I never pushed *her* into having to make a decision.

Most importantly, I stopped complaining that this manager was holding me back. I saw that I needed to build a relationship before she would invest time in me. Instead of trying to make her do her job or complaining about what she wasn't doing, I made her want to help me, want to promote me, want to give me more money. By the time my husband found a new job in Northern California, I had made myself so valuable to her that she suggested I work from home remotely in the Bay Area and commute to Los Angeles and NYC as needed. If we were still having those tense five-minute conversations, she easily could have used my move as a reason to part ways. Instead, I stayed in my role remotely for more than a year before pursuing a career change.

The point is, if you love your job and the company but hate your boss, determine if you are contributing to the friction and think about adjustments you can make while still being successful in your role. You can be the person to blame others or you can look honestly at whether you are self-sabotaging yourself or your relationship. If your boss is nice enough to give you feedback, listen. I "heard" my boss at Viacom telling me to change my personality and soften up, but that's not what she said. Her words were closer to, "You need to spend some time building relationships." Even that made me bristle. "Her relationships are better than mine?" I steamed. "That doesn't mean I don't have relationships!" When I finally took a moment and stepped back from the conversation, I was able to figure out what she was trying to say in her Amiable, non-confrontational, cryptic sort of way: It's not about the work. Build relationships outside of the day-to-day tasks. I did have relationships with people but only as they drove the work; they weren't "real" relationships. And she was right; relationships are everything in business.

So, listen, listen, and listen some more. What you learn may even elevate you to the next level. Make an effort to understand your boss's approach, even if he or she is less than clear. Looking back at the friction I had with my boss at Viacom, if I had listened better and been more self-aware, I'd have picked up on her messages much sooner. Bosses certainly aren't perfect, and if yours has trouble communicating, try to be more open to understanding. Ask questions. Be patient. If your boss betrayed you in some way, read the book *Rebuilding Trust in the Workplace: Seven Steps to Renew Confidence, Commitment, and Energy* by Dr. Dennis and Dr. Michelle Reina. If listening closely or reading that book doesn't work and you have no other solution, it may be time to move on.

2. Do I love my job but the company or team I work for is toxic? There are situations when you simply won't be able to work well with your boss or fix the company or the culture. If you love your job, but you think the team or company culture is toxic, first look at your words and actions and whether you are contributing to the toxicity. Are you gossiping or complaining? That will never help you get ahead nor is it a solution. In fact, by participating in gossip, you are part of the problem and creating more toxicity. Remove yourself from such behavior by asking anyone who tries to gossip with you, "Do you want me to listen or are you looking for some advice?" By giving them such options, you will let them know that you are willing to help but not interested in merely gossip.

The same applies to complaining. Complaining only adds to toxicity as opposed to problem-solving, which will get you noticed in a more positive way. Are you a worker bee focused only on the day-to-day tasks or are you thinking strategically and seeking ways to move the business forward to a higher level? Are you the one who comes up with great ideas but you are frustrated when they aren't all immediately implemented? Do you withhold information from others? Even when working in a toxic environment, you can succeed if you don't contribute to it. Consider your tone and attitude, your work product, and your overall demeanor. If you aren't part of the problem and you can't proactively help fix a toxic work environment, then it may be time to move on.

Note: There is no excuse for harassment, bullying, or discrimination of any kind. Report those situations to the head of HR and do your best to stay away from any perpetrators until the situation can be dealt with.

3. Have I become too complacent about what I do even though I can't see myself in this career for the next 20–30 years? You go to work every day and it's fine. It's a job. It pays the bills. It's good enough. But when you look at the next 10, 20, or 30 years of your life, can you continue to wash, rinse, and repeat? Imagine yourself ten years from now and what it will be like to walk into the same office, doing the same job, asking the same questions, and getting the same answers. If the answer is, "It won't bother me. I'll be just as content then as I am now," then keep doing it! If the answer is "I can't see myself doing this" and you are looking for more, then it may be time to consider what else is out there that would excite you every day.

That's what Marianne Lettieri did. I met her while flying from Dallas to San Jose. She was reading the book *The Artists Way: A Spiritual Path to Higher Creativity* by Julia Cameron. We started talking and she said she was heading to the San Jose Museum of Quilts and Textiles to install her latest art exhibition, "The Never-Ending Thread." The arc of her life is the perfect example of "no excuses." She went from a high-powered job at Apple to dumpster diving, and every word of her story will inspire you not to give in to your fears. Dumpster diving a good thing? Yes. Let me explain.

Marianne graduated college with a BA in Fine Arts and went to work for advertising and public relations agencies in Florida, eventually moving to Silicon Valley. After gaining years of experience and consulting for numerous tech companies, she became the manager of Corporate PR for Apple. It was the late '80s and tech was on fire. She remembers driving down the freeway thinking about her job. "I was like, all right, I made it! I can't believe I'm doing this. We really believed we were changing the world. It was an exciting time." Years later, while juggling her high-profile job and a four-year-old, her husband secured a job in the Netherlands. By then she was burned out. "I needed a break." So she went to Europe and took a two-year sabbatical.

When she came back to the U.S., Apple came calling and offered her a full-time role, but she wanted more control of her time. She agreed to work as an independent consultant for Apple but for other companies as well and did so for eight years. As those years passed, her work became less interesting and more stressful. At the same time, she was doing some freelance PR and communications work with public schools in Atherton, California, where her son was enrolled. As she got more involved, the more she enjoyed being involved with the community, creating something from nothing. That work reinvigorated the artist in her and her creative side came alive.

Soon she realized she had something to say and she wanted to express it in art. "The artist which had been lying dormant since I was 20 had to be free to create." She left Apple for good in her late 40s and started taking art classes at Stanford. She vividly remembers the experience: "I was going to be an artist again. I just knew it." She immersed herself in classes and people. "I was really excited, really passionate. It was filling me up, setting me on fire!" But saying she would be an artist was easier than creating a new identity and career.

Marianne had to learn a completely new infrastructure and develop new relationships in the art world. But she didn't have a network and didn't know how galleries worked. She also didn't have a title. Most people define themselves with a title and so had she, but now that she was no longer a PR manager or "worked in PR," she had to build a new identity for herself.

Initially, she decided to focus on decorative art. Her first job? Murals on people's walls inside their homes. She also painted a set of children's furniture for a VP at Apple. It was business. It was about making money. She used these jobs to financially survive. But she wanted to be a fine artist.

She saved her money and decided to go back to school, get a master's in fine arts, and beef up her fabrication skills (working with wood, metal, and glass). She also needed to learn the lingo of the art world and explain the conceptual underpinning of her art. Most people get their MFA to teach, but Marianne was there "to suck the bone marrow out of the school's fabrication facilities and contemporary art discourse."

She built a fine arts website and, not long after, won a contract from Oracle creating triptychs (three pictures next to each other) made from Sun Microsystems components. That meant dumpster diving in the company's trash! She made numerous triptychs for executive offices, and that contract alone paid for her MFA.

She's now into her 60s but you'd never know it; her energy and passion could surpass any college graduate. When I asked if she regretted spending so much time in PR or leaving PR, she paused to think. "I flip back and forth on that. If I'd stayed in PR, maybe I'd be a VP. And if I stayed with art right from college, maybe I'd be showing at the Venice Biennale or Art Basel. That's one of the trade-offs when flipping careers. It's hard to reach the top when you keep moving around. But I've progressed quickly in art because I know how to market, do spreadsheets, run a business, network, and speak in front of groups, and that came from PR. What I learned from one career translated well in this one. Maturity, knowledge, and experience also helped." She has one strong piece of advice for anyone contemplating changing careers: "If you are going to do it, do it hard. That's how I've gotten to where I am today."

And where is she? She's exhibited at the San Francisco Museum of Craft and Design, Monterey Peninsula College, Peninsula Museum of Art in Burlingame, Azusa Pacific University, and the San Jose Museum of Quilts and Textiles, to name a few. She won the 2017 Silicon Valley Laureate award for exceptional achievements in arts and contribution to the cultural life in Silicon Valley, which validated the hard work it took to transform into a recognized artist. She now teaches at art retreats and continues to hone her craft. Her title? Artist. "It was hard to say at first because I didn't believe it at first. It took a good year or two before I could say I'm an artist." Now she not only says it; she lives it, breathes it, works very hard at it, and loves every minute of it.

If you know your current job isn't forever or won't take you to retirement, now is the time to make a change. Don't wait another five years or two years or even one year to begin the transition. Don't let things like money or fear stop you. There is always a way, and you may even change again as you mature in your career.

4. Do I hate my job (or been fired) and want a completely new career but have no idea what I want to do? Sitting in a job you hate, toiling day after day for a paycheck, gets old for most people. Research has found that the average person spends 90,000 hours at work over a lifetime. Payscale. com says people spend approximately 13 years of their lives at work.[2] It seems reasonable to conclude that how you spend your days at work will affect your home life. Hating your work when you spend most of your time there can't possibly have a positive effect on your quality of life.

For some, being fired—even from a job they loved—was the best thing that ever happened because it forced them to look beyond their current career track. Just ask David Gonzalez, who has always had insatiable curiosity. Growing up as the son of immigrant parents who never graduated from high school, he saw how hard they worked to build their auto mechanic shop. He had graduated from high school and was taking college classes while working at his parents' shop when he turned pro as a dirt bike racer. He made the Top 10 in both Motocross and Supercross and life seemed on track. Then it happened: He suffered a major injury, forcing him out of competition.

"It felt like I was fired. My initial reaction was, 'What am I going to do and how am I going to do it?' I had just come off my best year and was in the best shape of my life." He hoped he could continue racing after recovering from his injuries, but his momentum would be lost. "What am I going to do?" kept gnawing at him. "If I don't get off this track right now," he recalled thinking, "I will miss other opportunities even though I didn't know what those were."

David finished college with a BA in Criminal Justice and thought he would apply for a job at the FBI or DEA. But after talking to some agents who brought their cars to his dad's shop, he realized such work wouldn't be as exciting or interesting as he thought. A college professor recommended he meet a man who owned an ad agency and was looking to market to the Hispanic and Latino community. David met him and was offered a job to help build that part of the agency's business. He moved to San Antonio and worked on major accounts like Coca-Cola and Bud Light for Sosa, Bromley, Aguilar & Associates, which at the time was the largest ad agency in the country.

After working there for four years, he realized he wanted more but didn't know what that was until he saw an advertisement for a conference called the Creative Problem-Solving Institute. It sounded interesting so he decided to check it out. On the last day, he describes sitting and talking to another attendee when a book fell out of the attendee's bag. It was from a master's degree program at SUNY Buffalo on Creativity and Change

Leadership, and that led to a conversation between them about the book. In that moment, David felt more curious than he had ever been. Even though he was making more money than he could ever imagine and was at the top of his game in advertising, he went back to work on Monday, quit his job, and then moved to Buffalo to start the program.

"Sure, it's easier to take risks when you're single," he said. "It gets more complicated when you have a family and kids. But if you don't take risks because of fear or you don't know what you want to do, you are giving up on your potential." David attributes his ability to change course in his career to his insatiable curiosity. "What's possible? Life is too short, as they say. It's full of too much potential. Why do the same thing when you don't have to? It's a mindset more than anything. Do I want to stay on one track or explore multiple tracks that will take me to all kinds of destinations?"

David has since earned a PhD in Performance Improvement and worked at numerous companies providing customized talent development, leadership, and organizational effectiveness solutions. He has also lived in multiple states, including California, where he took a job at Juniper Networks in the Human Resources department. Prior to that, he had never worked in Human Resources. While managing the illness of a family member for many years, he made yet another change: taking a job at Intuitive Surgical even though he had never worked at a medical technology company.

"I'd been dealing with this challenging family situation and I was afraid of another change and how much harder it could make my life . . . the new people, new relationships, having to prove myself. That would be tiring under any other circumstance, though a healthy family would have made it easier." Still, he made the move because he realized he couldn't stay in the role he was in. "I got to the place where I thought, I can't have everything in my life be challenging. If my personal life was going to continue to be challenging, I want some abundance on the professional side. I want to be playful and creative with good people around me and this new role would provide that."

Is this David's last career change? Probably not, he said. He still has that insatiable curiosity and has since bought property in Spain and Italy with a dream of moving into real estate someday . . . or something else. He remains open to possibilities. "I think the Imposter Syndrome creeps in when people think about changing careers. 'Will I be good at this?' they wonder. Whenever I changed directions, I would have these conversations with the Universe: You better have my back!" He chuckles, but, as a talent development expert, he knows that curiosity is the start to any great career.

5. Do I know what I want to do but have no experience doing it? You may not have worked in the new career, but you do have experience that relates to it. Every job you have ever held has provided you with foundational knowledge, hard skills, and soft skills, all of which are experience. The goal is to learn how those skills directly transfer to the new career. When I moved into Human Resources at the age of 47, I had never worked in HR, but my experience in TV news made me a great communicator, my experience as a lawyer helped me master influencing, and my experience working in production risk gave me experience aligning people (reality show participants) with company goals (high ratings). Every experience you have had can be framed through the lens of the new job. You just need to know how to do that. You've come to the right place.

6. Am I in high school or college or about to graduate and still haven't figured out what I want to do? How lucky you are! Your entire life is ahead of you and you are reading this book to learn that whatever first job you take, it doesn't have to be your final career choice. Find your first job and take things from there. You will learn and gain skills no matter what you do. This book will help you position and leverage those skills when you figure out what you want to do—next.

If you are still in school, now is the time to take internships. I am always stunned when I hear my friends tell me their college-age children aren't interning during their college summers. I often wonder what they will put on their resumes when they graduate. College is a glorious time to learn at a higher level, make new friends, do your own laundry for the first time, and have fun. It is also a time to figure out what you will do when you graduate.

When my friends and I interned, we worked for free; today, most interns are paid. Internships don't just help you figure out what you may want to do; they also help you to determine what you don't want to do. I was mentoring a young woman, Annie, who wanted to go into marketing. She took an internship at a public TV and radio station in the marketing department. She doubted she wanted to work at a TV/radio station but knew that the value of a first internship is getting some work experience. And she did, gaining substantive skills in departmental collaboration, project management, data forecasting, and writing. It was a valuable internship, but it also convinced her that she didn't want to work in nonprofits or public television.

Her second internship was working in ad sales marketing. She spent most of her days on PowerPoint presentations and Request for Proposal responses to help drive ad revenue. She grew her cross-functional communication skills while working with multiple teams to develop effective sales pitch materials. She joined brainstorming sessions to determine go-to-market strategies for new products. She expanded her data skills using data sets from Nielsen, eMarketer, Tableau, and Salesforce. She liked the job and loved the company but still wasn't sure it was the kind of marketing she wanted to pursue after graduating from college.

During her final year at school she decided to get yet another internship. This time she wanted to try the agency side so she secured a position with a smaller company that would give her more exposure to public relations. While working on publicity campaigns for the agency's clients, she picked up skills in Search Engine Optimization to increase engagement on social media and increase subscriber and visitor traffic to client websites. She also continued to hone her writing skills while starting a blog on topics in the consumer technology space. And she expanded her knowledge of performance marketing while analyzing reports using Google Analytics. With just six months to graduate, she decided to start her career at an agency knowing it probably wouldn't be a long-term career choice.

Every internship she had was a successful experience because she kept narrowing down what she wanted to do and what she didn't want to do. Parts of her internships helped her decide that she still wanted to work in marketing, but she hadn't found her niche. When she graduated from college, she had two offers: one from a large, well-known agency and one from a smaller company she had interned with. She weighed both offers and chose ad sales marketing because it would help evolve her writing and integrated marketing skills even though she wasn't sure it would be her "forever" job.

For those of you with no idea what to do, seek out internships in various fields. You may love some and hate others, but you will learn enough to figure out what career direction makes the most sense. Most companies won't hire someone as an intern who is no longer enrolled in college. If you're unemployed, consider registering for a night course in the field you want to move into. That way you are "in school" and can obtain an internship during the day.

Chapter 1 Summary

1. **Love your job but hate your boss:** Determine your role in the relationship and whether you can alter your behavior to make it work better. If you've been given feedback about your hard or soft skills, seek to understand it deeply, and create and implement an action plan. If the relationship still doesn't change, life is too short. Keep reading this book and move on!

2. **Love your job but the company/team is toxic:** Look at your actions and determine if you are joining in others' bad behavior. Can you change the team behavior through example? If not, move on. If you see behavior that constitutes harassment or other illegal behavior, report it to Human Resources.

3. **Complacent for now but won't be happy doing your role in 10, 20, 30 years:** Don't wait to look ahead at your life and determine whether you can do the same job in a decade or two

from now. If your current job isn't forever or won't take you to retirement, now is the time to consider how to gain skills to make that transition.

4. **Hate your job and want a new career but don't know what you want to do:** The main skill you need to figure out what you want to do is curiosity. Being open to any and all possibilities, no matter how different from your current role, will allow you to explore possibilities and find the right job and career for you.

5. **College grad or graduating soon and no idea what you want to do:** If you are still in school, now is the time to take internships, which will help you determine jobs you want and don't want to do. If you've graduated and are unemployed, consider registering for a night community college course in the field you may want to move into; that way you are still learning in school and can obtain an internship during the day.

2

Assessing What's Important to You

"It's not hard to make decisions when you know what your values are."

—Roy Disney, co-founder, The Walt Disney Company

How many times have you made a list of pros and cons before making an important decision? We may come up with more pros or more cons to skew the choice, but it will still have to be made, and sometimes it will go against what the list seems to say. Don't worry. This chapter won't suggest that you write such a list for various career choices. Those lists are nice, but they don't say what you truly need to know. All they reveal is what you like and don't like about your current or prospective position. Instead, take a step back and evaluate more deeply what drives you in life and in the workplace.

Before making any decision, especially one as important as your career, it's best to first identify and understand your values. The Co-Active Training Institute is a professional coach training and certification program that has trained more than 65,000 coaches, including employees in a third of the Fortune 100 companies. Co-Active teaches, "Our values serve as a compass pointing out what it means to be true to oneself. When we honor our values on a regular and consistent basis, life is good and fulfilling."[1] Simply put: Making career changes or life decisions based on

Tip #2: Understand your values to determine what you want in a career.

external pressures or without identifying and understanding your values could lead to impulsivity, faulty assumptions, and/or set-ups for failure. I'm sure you know a few people who jump from one bad relationship to the next. They probably never took the time to think about what is truly important to them. They are only interested in getting out of a bad situation or "showing someone" they found something better. If you don't think about your values, each relationship is compared to the one before without the wisdom of knowing whether these "significant others" were able to provide something truly important and meaningful. One relationship may seem "better" than the last one but not for long because they aren't filling most or all your core values.

The same goes for job seekers. Have you jumped from one bad job to the next? There's a chance you were looking to "just get out" of a bad situation or maybe you jumped for a higher title or more money instead of a position that would truly satisfy all of your values. If you understand your values and live them at work, you will be happy and fulfilled, more engaged and productive.

Values change throughout our lives, so doing a values exercise provides a helpful snapshot of what they are in a given moment in time. Identifying your values on your own requires some deep thought and self-awareness. I always recommend working with a coach because she or he will help you uncover values you may not realize you have or didn't realize were actually values. That said, if hiring a coach is not an option, I suggest starting with "likes and dislikes" and using those as a stepping stone to help you identify your core values.

Likes and Dislikes

How did you land in your current job or career? Did you graduate college with no idea what to do and fell into it? Did you target a job or career and now you're moving up the ladder? Think about the job you have or previous jobs (or internships for those in college). What do/did you like about it/them? What don't/didn't you like? Now don't say, "I hate my job." (Caught you!) If you've been in a job or career for a while, there must be something you like about it. For example, even in previous jobs I "hated,"

I liked . . .

→ being independent.

→ making an impact and feeling valued for it.

→ making independent decisions without a lot of oversight.

→ bosses who didn't micromanage.

→ cross-collaborating across multiple business units.

→ managing and mentoring others early in their career.

→ expanding my knowledge and constantly learning.

→ owning projects from beginning to end.

Just like figuring out what you like about your job, now figure out what you don't/didn't like about it/them.

For example, I disliked . . .

→ that toward the end of nearly every job, I wasn't learning.

→ doing a job on autopilot (boredom).

→ having to be something or someone I'm not to "fit in."

→ working for a hierarchical company.

→ that in certain jobs, I didn't click with my boss as much as I wanted to.

→ companies that weren't transparent with information such as company goals.

→ watching constant changes being made with no idea why.

→ feeling undervalued because my pay was not at the level the company would need to replace me or what the company was paying others at my level.

→ the red tape and roadblocks when I was trying to move fast.

→ working with "no, but" people and not "yes, and" people.

→ working with "B-list" or "C-list" people who were coasting and ineffective but were promoted or moved to other roles instead of terminated.

If you have trouble thinking about what you like or dislike about your work, think about a time when you were happy and productive or sad, frustrated, and angry. What made you feel such emotion? Now think about a time you felt complacent. What made you feel that way? Once you finish your list, it's time to figure out your values in relation to work.

Values = What Is Important to You

How do "likes and dislikes" correspond with values? They identify what you feel is important, and once you know that, you can match them with core values. Again, it's easier to work with a coach, but without one, you can Google "core values list" to help kick off your thoughts. A more comprehensive list can also be found in "values cards."[2] I'm not a huge fan of these lists or cards because they are limited and won't always represent deeper impulses, but they will get you thinking and that's what is most important.

No matter what method you use, choosing values that truly represent who YOU are at your core is critical in this exercise. Some people will have 20 values. Some will have five. The number doesn't matter; picking *true* values does. Some people will try to be virtuous or pick values they think they should have or wish they had. For example, consider the value "learning new things." Some people love to learn something new. Bill Gates reportedly reads about a book a week![3] Now let's take "John," who is exploring his core values. John admires Bill Gates and wishes he could read and absorb as much information as Gates does. John thus may think that "learning" is one of his core values. He should always want to learn, and he certainly has a desire to. But if John is given a choice between watching *Seinfeld* reruns, reading a book, visiting a museum, or watching a documentary, he will choose *Seinfeld* every time. While John likes to learn and learning seems like a "good" or "socially acceptable" value, it's not his burning desire or even something he seeks out every day. If John believes that "learning" is a value, he will need to define it clearly to know what that means to him because it won't mean the same thing as what it means to Bill Gates. It also may not be as important a value as other values because it isn't something that brings him joy and fulfills him each day.

If you are self-aware enough to stop yourself from choosing values you *want* to have or *wish* you had or *seem* like the right values to have, you will be able to define those *true* values that will help you make decisions about your career and future. From your likes and dislikes, you are now prepared to identify some values. Here's what I did with my likes/dislikes list:

What I like	Corresponding value
Being independent	Freedom to make decisions
Making an impact and feeling valued for it	Impact and recognition
Cross-collaborating across multiple business units	Teamwork
Managing and mentoring others early in their career	Teaching
Accomplishing projects from beginning to end	Following through on work to completion
What I dislike	**Corresponding value**
That I wasn't learning anymore toward the end of each job	Taking on work outside my comfort zone
That I could do the job on autopilot/boredom	Diversity of tasks
Not having to be something I'm not to fit in	Authenticity
Working for a hierarchical company	Equality
Didn't click with my boss	Relationships
Companies that weren't transparent with information / constant change with no understanding of why	Direct access to senior leaders
Pay was less than others	Feeling valued
Red tape and roadblocks	Being efficient
Working with "no but" people instead of "yes, and" people	Working with enthusiastic, solution-oriented people
Working with people who were coasting and ineffective	Working with smart people

You may be thinking, "Yes, those are my values, too!" But even if we have the same values or likes and dislikes, it doesn't mean they represent the same things. Why? Because each of those words could mean different things to different people. For example, if "flexibility" was one of my values, it would mean that I can attend my kids' school concerts or special activities and stop work by 5 p.m. most nights so I can be home for a family dinner. "Flexibility" to someone else may mean working from home one day a week. Therefore, it's critical to extrapolate what each identified value means to you.

The Co-Active Coaching Toolkit explains how to create a value string. Use a "stream of consciousness" (unedited brainstorming) approach to write down what comes to mind about each value with a slash between each thought. You aren't striving for perfection here. Value strings don't have to be in complete sentences. You are defining what the value means to you with either words or examples. Here are a few value strings:

- ➜ **Freedom to make decisions:** not being micromanaged / making strategic decisions / being able to decide the order of my work / not being "minded" or "looked after" / owning my work wholly and separately from my boss / flexibility to come and go from work as I need to be successful

- ➜ **Teamwork:** working closely with others / learning about others' needs / working across several areas / influencing others / new perspectives / diversity of thought

- ➜ **Teaching:** helping others raise their star / influencing younger generations / giving information I wish I had at their age / helping others see different perspectives / helping others learn / feeling needed

- ➜ **Following through on work to completion:** sense of "Yay, I did it!" / sense of finishing something / a checkbox to get it off my plate / feeling valued / feeling productive / feeling that I know I'm needed / working on the big, impactful project, not the minutiae

→ **Authenticity:** no backstabbing / people care about each other / no secrets / being myself around others and still being liked and valued / mean what you say and say what you mean / no "air" about you / self-aware / saying what you mean and meaning what you say

→ **Direct access to senior leaders:** being part of the decision-making process / being part of the big picture / working with the top leaders of a company / never wondering why a decision was made / being in the know

→ **Feeling valued:** paid what I'm worth / know that others believe I am worth what I believe I am worth / someone saying "thank you" or "I couldn't have done this without you" / someone saying "good job" / having a boss invest in me and my future

→ **Being efficient:** getting stuff done without roadblocks / making informed decisions quickly / pushing things forward / not being stalled / checking the box on work and move it off my desk / accomplishing something

→ **Working with smart people:** learning from others / not being the smartest person in the room / being the dumbest person in the room / every meeting is an opportunity to learn / feeling mentally challenged daily / being uncomfortable / feeling pushed to be better

Sometimes your stream of consciousness will lead you to more values that will require a new stream of consciousness. Break them out and do the same exercise. Once you have all your value strings, narrow each one down to the descriptor or definition that resonates the most. From the above list, mine looks like this:

→ **Freedom to make decisions** = owning my work wholly and separately from my boss

→ **Teamwork** = working across several areas

→ **Teaching** = helping others raise their star

→ **Following through on work to completion** = working on the big, impactful project, not the minutiae

→ **Authenticity** = mean what you say and say what you mean

→ **Direct access to senior leaders** = being in the know

→ **Feeling valued** = paid what I'm worth

→ **Being efficient** = getting stuff done without roadblocks

→ **Working with smart people** = feeling mentally challenged daily

Then, rank each value from 1 to 10 on your current job or past jobs overall:

1 You don't have it in your job at all.

10 You have it in your job every day.

Here is what my job at Viacom looked like by the time I was ready to leave:

→ (6) **Freedom to make decisions** = owning my work wholly and separately from my boss

→ (4) **Teamwork** = working across several areas

→ (8) **Teaching** = helping others raise their star

→ (4) **Following through on work to completion** = working on the big, impactful project, not the minutiae

→ (7) **Authenticity** = mean what you say and say what you mean

→ (3) **Direct access to senior leaders** = being in the know

→ (1) **Feeling valued** = paid what I'm worth

→ (4) **Being efficient** = getting stuff done without roadblocks

→ (2) **Working with smart people** = feeling mentally challenged daily

When I evaluated Viacom through this lens of values, I realized that many ranked below a 5 and the job no longer fit my values. I say "no longer" because many of those values were a 10 when I started.

Some of them either no longer mattered or I hadn't identified them as values when I took the job, but they became that way in the course of my work. Many times, our values change as we grow. What we want when we are 20 may be quite different than when we are 50. What we want before we have children could change after we have children. What we want when we move into a new job could be hugely different after we've been there for a while. When I took the job at Viacom, I wanted my VP stripes (title), more money (paid for value), and more responsibility (scope). I was also learning daily and managing a larger team. My values were fulfilled when I started the job, but six years later, a lot had changed.

It may seem obvious that with so many low numbers, leaving my job would be a no-brainer, but that's not necessarily true for everyone. If you have low numbers and still like the company you work for, determine whether you can find a way to live your values in your current job. For example, if you love working on strategic projects but don't have the time, can you find another way to make room for them? Have you built good relationships with strategic leaders? Will your boss support you? There are likely some options, but it may take some work.

Is it realistic to find a job that meets ALL your values? It is, but again, you have to invest some time. Too many people settle for the "next step up" or are running away from a bad situation and don't evaluate whether that next step will deliver what's important to them. And work values are not the only component to figuring out which job fits you best; you also need to consider personal values. Here are some of mine:

- → **Short commute** = no longer than 30 minutes is ideal; more than 40 is a deal-breaker
- → **Must have daily interaction with others** = being around people either in person or via video conference
- → **Meaningful travel** = for *real* reasons, not just to "make an appearance" somewhere
- → **No completely open floor plan** = cubicles and offices are fine but no long tables

➜ **No pets in office** = no dogs or iguanas (common in the Bay Area!)

➜ **Work/life balance** = Flexible arrival/departure (not clocking in or out) and able to attend kids' events (school concerts, parades, etc.)

➜ **Vacation time** = minimum 20 days/year (can start at 15 days + holidays as long as it moves to 20 days within two years) or unlimited Paid Time Off.

You may also have values about size of the company: Small or big? How about industry? Healthcare, tech, entertainment, financial? Does the company need to be "sexy"? Do you want to read about it in the news? And location? Are you willing to move to a new city? If so, are there limits on where? Your list should be much longer than the example above.

By now you're probably thinking, "Yeah, this is a nice dream. Wish me luck finding everything I want.... I never said you'd match *every* value, but there is no harm in trying.

It's also helpful to look at needs versus wants. After identifying your values, separate them into three groups:

➜ Critical ("Must have")

➜ Important ("Nice to have")

➜ Optional ("Not as important")

When I was looking to transition to the role of HR business partner, I interviewed at a well-known Silicon Valley tech company where I had to make a presentation to a group of four women. Two of them were each hiring for that position—one to support the Emerging Business department and one to support the General Counsel. I figured I was a lawyer and prepared to transition into Human Resources, so I was perfect for at least the General Counsel support role.

As I dove into the presentation—a business problem I discovered and solved using data—the hiring manager representing emerging businesses asked me about a time when I helped *drive* business. Unfortunately, my answer was more about making sure business could continue versus driving it forward. My Viacom job was about "getting to yes" and putting safeguards in place when "yes" was risky. I could tell by the interviewer's tone and her repeating the question that she was frustrated with my answer. I knew I'd blown it but hoped I still had a chance to impress the other manager who was hiring for the General Counsel.

Since I had always worked on the business side and not the HR side, I didn't understand how such interview panels worked and that they would collectively decide if I was a fit for a role and the company. When the second hiring manager asked me a question about how my current role was relevant to the open role supporting the General Counsel, I saw the first hiring manager roll her eyes. I was shocked but answered the question as best I could.

The day went from bad to worse when the first hiring manager met with me separately. She arrived late and was texting on her phone the entire time while explaining that she was coordinating her son's birthday party that night. Clearly, she had decided I wasn't a good fit for the team and company, and I was just as clear in my head that she wasn't the right boss for me. Then she excused herself early from the interview and someone else not on the interview schedule came in. I continued to be polite and express my interest in the role. That said, my interest waned further when the commute home from Mountain View at 5 p.m. took 80 minutes—twice my deal-breaker of 40 minutes.

It would have made sense, of course, to call the recruiter and immediately pull out of the running. But I did the exact opposite. I went home, told my husband the story, and then let my brain "swirl" for a while. I started thinking, "I'm transitioning careers and it will be hard going from lawyer to HR business partner, so if I get this, I'll take it because I can always leave in a year if it doesn't work out." And then I thought, "I have to start somewhere. I'll take the first thing I get and deal with it." My final thought: "Anything is better than where I'm at." I had talked myself into *needing* this job, even though I was disrespected during the interview process and the commute was longer than 40 minutes. The entire experience violated my values.

The next day the recruiter called to inform me I didn't get either job. I was professional on the phone, asked a few questions, and learned it was because of that one question I didn't answer well. My heart fell. Rejection sucks even if you know the job isn't right for you. But I still wasn't willing to let go. I sent the recruiter a note thanking her again for the opportunity and that I was disappointed the team didn't feel I was the right fit for either role. Then I wrote:

> *My tenacity, of course, screams, "Wait!" While I respect and understand the team's needs, I wanted to make sure that their decision was not based on a simple miscommunication on my part which may have arisen in my last interview.*

I wrote three more paragraphs about how I could leverage my experience to drive business, answering the question via email that I failed answering in the room. I ended the email with this:

> *If, in light of the above, either team expresses any interest in continuing our conversation, please let them know that I'd welcome the opportunity. Either way, I want you to know that I truly appreciate everyone's time and I'd love to be considered when there are other opportunities at your company. From all I learned during the process and the people I have met along the way, I am even more impressed with your company.*

Looking back, I think, *How embarrassing.* Not because I threw myself at their mercy or felt humiliated about what I wrote, but because I completely ignored my values. I wanted so badly to get my foot in the door and transition careers that I was ignoring what was profoundly important to me and fighting for a job and a situation that was so wrong for me. I wasn't focused on my core values. If I was, I would have written a thank-you note that expressed my gratitude but also stated it wasn't the right fit for me. Of course, the recruiter never wrote back. I learned from the experience to never let my desire to move into a new career drive me to ignore my core values.

Within weeks I was interviewing at Roku, where I was treated great during the interview process and the commute was only ten minutes. I *really* wanted this job and changed my thinking and approach. I reviewed my values every time I came home from interviews. I believed I could hit 10s or close to 10 for every value. After I was hired (Yay!), I evaluated whether the actual working environment was as I'd predicted based on the interviews. It was remarkably close.

The best part of taking a new job is you learn more about yourself and discover some values you didn't list. For example, I never cared about the size of the company I worked for. That changed while working at Roku. It had about 500 employees when I was hired and 1,200 by the time I left and I loved that. Most of the companies I worked for had more than 10,000 employees worldwide. So I have a new value: working for a company under 5,000 people. I also learned that I had a value about transparency. Remember that I disliked watching my work environment change and not knowing why? It happened a lot, and so I added transparency as a value and to always "be in the know" at the highest levels of a company.

Chapter 2 Summary

1. **What do you value?** If you understand your values and live them at work, you will be happy and fulfilled, more engaged and productive. Determine what is important to you in a workplace and in life through a values exercise.

2. **Define your values.** Defining your values is not hard, but it does take time to zero in on exactly what is important to you and how important each value is to you. Creating values strings will help you hone further what your values truly mean.

3. **Your values are unique to you.** Be careful not to be virtuous or pick values you think you should have or wish you had or your friends have. Your values are unique to you and only you know

what is truly important to you. Once you define your values, you will use them to guide you to either improve your current work situation or find a career that best fulfills you.

4. **Rank your values.** Ranking your values from 1–10 will allow you to see where you can improve your current work experience or help you define which values are most important if you can't find a job that satisfies all of your values.

3

What Do You Want to Do?

"The great secret of getting what you want from life is to know what you want and believe you can have it."

—Norman Vincent Peale, minister and author

Now that you know how to determine if your current job is aligned with your values, you hopefully have a better understanding of how to create more 10s or whether it's time to find a new job. You can also use values to evaluate a new career. When I changed careers/companies from Viacom lawyer to Roku Human Resources Business Partner, I received dozens of emails from people asking me, "How did you do that?" I said, "I made a decision to change careers and then I figured out how to do it." Sounds easy, right? But no transition is that simple.

At the beginning I felt lost. I had panic attacks. I didn't want to keep doing what I was doing but I had no idea what I wanted to do. After a week of turmoil, I realized that my complaining was stressing me out and wasn't helping me to move forward. What did help was reviewing my values and confirming why my level of fulfillment was so low. Managing production risk on reality shows is unique and, in my mind at the time, didn't relate to many other jobs in the market. I'd either have to commit to this unique role with minimum salary increases for the next 20+ years until retirement or figure out how to make the skills

Tip #3: Figure out what skills you have that excite you to narrow down prospective career choices.

I'd obtained relate to some other field. Twenty years seemed like a long time to be bored.

Hard and Soft Skills

The number one reason people seek me out as a career coach is because they have no idea what they want to do. They have been in a career for 10, 20, 30 years and they hate it. They are more than ready to leave but don't know how to transition their current skills into another field. Or they know of a few careers where their skills are transferrable but have no interest in them. "What do I want to do?" is a really hard question to answer. What new role can use their skills as well as meet their values?

All the skills you use at work are either "hard" or "soft." Hard skills are easier to measure and teach such as analyzing information, processing payroll, or programming. Certain levels and experience in hard skills are needed for each specific job. Most of the time, if a person has some hard skills but needs to learn others to be a perfect match for a role, a company will look at your capacity to learn and grow. For example, if someone is smart and has learned five kinds of coding programs on their own, some companies may believe he or she can easily adapt to a new kind of computer programming. If someone has experience analyzing financial data but not Human Resources data, a company may believe that the person can apply the same analytic skills to a different set of data.

Soft skills, by comparison, aren't used in a specific job; they are needed for every job. Soft skills are just as important, if not more important, than hard skills in most jobs.[1] They sound like "emotional intelligence," "able to influence," and "interpersonal skills." They define one's ability to act, communicate, and adapt. Soft skills will distinguish higher performers from lower performers and higher productivity from lower productivity. For example, someone with a high level of emotional intelligence will know how to influence without jamming ideas down others' throats. They are able to truly listen to others, be self-aware about their own faults and mistakes, and react to stressful situations in ways that don't threaten productivity or forward movement. Someone with low emotional intelligence will create perpetuate swirl or conflict, make others around them feel unheard and/or unappreciated, and alienate others from wanting to work for them or even the company. They likely aren't even aware of their negative impact. This type of behavior ultimately leads to lower productivity.

The annual "Future of Jobs Report" from the World Economic Forum shows how soft skills have evolved since 2015. You will notice that some of the top skills needed in the 2020 workforce weren't even considered in 2015.

Top 10 Skills in 2015	Top 10 Skills in 2020
1. Complex Problem-Solving	1. Complex Problem-Solving
2. Coordinating with Others	2. Critical Thinking
3. People Management	3. Creativity
4. Critical Thinking	4. People Management
5. Negotiation	5. Coordinating with Others
6. Quality Control	6. Emotional Intelligence
7. Service Orientation	7. Judgment and Decision Making
8. Judgment and Decision Making	8. Service Orientation
9. Active Listening	9. Negotiation
10. Creativity	10. Cognitive Flexibility

Consider the first three top skills grouped together in 2020: Complex Problem-Solving, Critical Thinking, and Creativity. This means that managers no longer want you to bring them problems unless you've already worked through all possible solutions. They also want to know the risks of those solutions. They want to see that you aren't just "selling" your idea of what should be done but bringing thought leadership to every issue. If "complex problem-solving" is the number one skill valued in the workplace for the past five years, figuring out how it aligns with your values should be a top priority.

While Active Listening was in the Top 10 in 2015, it has evolved into Emotional Intelligence in 2020. And while it's "only" No. 6, Human Resources generally considers it No. 1 because it impacts People Management and Coordinating with Others. For those who don't know what Emotional Intelligence is or how to apply it for success in life and work,

I recommend the book *Emotional Intelligence 2.0* by Travis Bradberry and Jean Greaves. It will teach you such emotional intelligence skills as self-awareness, self-management, social awareness, and relationship management. You might be excellent at complex problem-solving or critical thinking, but if you don't know how to influence or communicate, it doesn't matter how good you are at other skills; you won't succeed long term at your company. At most companies, there is a lot less tolerance these days for the "brilliant jerk." Be sure to address emotional intelligence skills in your resume but also be sure you're good at them!

Finally, look at Cognitive Flexibility. What a great term for a resume! This wasn't even on the 2015 list but it goes well with Emotional Intelligence. Cognitive Flexibility means the ability to adapt to change and new environments. Companies are changing at a rapid pace, merging and consolidating functions and roles. If you have ever worked at a start-up, you get it. As start-ups add people, your scope of work narrows, and you're expected to go deeper into a specific area. Such employees need to enhance their subject matter expertise if they want to support a growing business—and stay employed! Further, they need to be able to adopt and adapt to change daily.

I worked at a company that went through three major reorganizations in two years. That's a lot of change. Managers lost their teams. Employees' roles were redefined. One manager was given three different charters and teams of people to manage and lost them just as fast, not because she was a bad manager but because the business was growing so fast that the structure needed to change to keep pace. The key to Cognitive Flexibility is whether you can adapt to the change. If you are still complaining a year later, you haven't. Also, when work is stressful, what happens to your productivity? If you have Cognitive Flexibility, you can shift your thinking from situation to situation and prevent stress or environmental changes from altering your effectiveness.

Translate Values into Hard and Soft Skills

If you don't know what other skills you have or enjoy using that are relevant to the role you seek, look back at your values. From those, identify specific hard and soft skills you use in your job or in previous jobs that reflect those values and align with a required skill. Here are a few examples of translating values into hard and soft work skills:

Value	Value Definition	Skill
Distilling / analyzing information	Using data to solve business problems and drive the business forward	**HARD:** Data analysis, using Visier and Tableau programs, providing data insights to drive business decisions **SOFT:** Detail oriented; working cross-functionally with business leaders; complex problem-solving
Teaching others	Helping others be the best they can be and raise their star	**HARD:** Being a subject matter expert on specific matters **SOFT:** Coaching/mentoring; being trustworthy
Project flexibility	Unpredictable/different projects every day	**HARD:** Subject matter expertise from knowledge and experience **SOFT:** Nimble/agile; able to adapt to change; multitask on multiple projects; confidence to find answers in any situation even if unfamiliar; complex problem-solving
Making decisions	Authority to own a project or process	**HARD:** Track record of sound decision making, which drives the business **SOFT:** Being strategic; working independently; respect from the team; complex problem-solving

Notice that the list above doesn't mention a specific field. There are numerous fields where these skills would be relevant and values would be fulfilled. In fact, most of the above skills are soft because, as mentioned, they are the skills that will bring you success or failure in any role. They will also be examined the hardest for "culture fit" during the interview process.

Identify Careers That Fit Your Values

Once you've identified your skills, it's time to start looking at careers that interest you and eliminate those that are clearly wrong. But first, one very important ground rule: While eliminating careers that are clearly wrong, make sure you don't make the critical mistake of eliminating a career based on your lack of experience in that field or lack of specialized education or concern about pay compared to your current salary. We will look at all those considerations later. This exercise is to eliminate careers that you truly know are wrong based on the career itself and/ or your interests based on your values. Also, eliminate careers that you don't have an interest in even though they might be obvious choices for your skill set.

For example, I knew I loved to help people, but I couldn't watch a medical show without closing my eyes or looking away during the surgery scenes. Being a nurse or doctor or pursuing any job that involved blood or bodily fluids daily was out. I enjoyed writing and I was good at synthesizing, but I can't do math that is more advanced than the basics, so while research and analysis interested me, any kind of number crunching was out. I loved screenwriting and had completed numerous screenplays, but I couldn't be a screenwriter full-time because one of my top values is stability and that means not having any debt. The screenwriters you hear about are the ones who broke through, but most don't, so it would remain a hobby.

Look Outside the Norm for Possibilities

Now that you've eliminated careers that aren't the right fit, it's time to figure out which ones are based on your values and hard and soft skills. This is where the panic sets in for most people. "But I don't know what's out there" is the lament I hear most often. That's right, you don't. But you do have access to unlimited free data on nearly every job that exists including ones you may have never heard of. Where to start? Here:

→ **The Bureau of Labor Statistics** (https://www.bls.gov/ooh/) breaks down each occupation group into fastest growing, highest pay, etc. It's a comprehensive list and you may find a career you didn't know existed or never would have thought of that may resonate with you.

→ **World Economic Forum** (www.weforum.org) provides articles on which job sectors are growing and will need workers in future years as well as jobs that may not exist yet but will. Review "The Future of Jobs" reports to find skills needed for all jobs and how in-demand skill sets have been evolving over the years.

→ **Associations.** If you're a whiz at social media and want a job in that field, go to SocialMedia.org and see what kinds of jobs exist and what is required to work in that field. If you're interested in HR, check out the Society for Human Resource Management (SHRM). Associations or groups that focus on one job or field have a plethora of information.

→ **College career sites.** If you graduated from college, don't hesitate to go back to your college career sites, but know that this is exploratory. If you graduated from the engineering or business school, do they have job postings? If you graduated from the communications program, what roles are posted? This is all about research and learning what exists that you may not know about.

→ **Boolean searching on Google.** A Boolean search lists multiple key words for skill areas with modifiers like "and," "or," or "but." Searching key words plus the word "jobs" will also give you an idea of what jobs and careers require your skill set. If I simply Google "coaching, analyzing complex issues, and writing," the search results in various articles about those subjects including one about HR and others about executive coaching, writing resumes, or career coaching (go figure!).

You can also try other more generic searches such as . . .

→ **"Best career for someone who enjoys . . . X"** If I replace X with "writing," there are a lot of results. One is a "trade schools" article (https://www.trade-schools.net/articles/jobs-for-writers .asp#jobs-for-writers), which has numerous careers I never would have thought of including grant writer, content strategist, speechwriter, technical writer, video game writer, social media specialist, web content writer, ghostwriter, and so on.

→ **"Most interesting careers"** for those of you looking for something entirely different nets another trade-schools.net article (https://www.trade-schools.net/articles/unique-careers.asp). A "Professional Bridesmaid"? Who would have thought that such a job existed!

→ **"Best Travel Jobs"** for those who want to see the world while working delivered an Expert Vagabond article (https://expert vagabond.com/best-travel-jobs/) and again, there were jobs I didn't even know existed. Then I remembered the three guides from Backroads (www.backroads.com) who led a bike trip I took from Prague to Vienna. One of them had visited more than 50 countries—some for work and some for fun—while traveling on his days off. I remember being instantly jealous that I hadn't thought about doing that in my 20s.

As you look through each job, take your pulse. Are you energized to learn more? Are you just lukewarm when you read the description? You are looking for careers that excite you and make you want to keep researching to learn more. I once coached a young woman named Lisa, who had a BA in Psychology and worked as a leasing/marketing coordinator and then a patient/surgical coordinator. She was no longer interested in either of them but had no idea what she wanted to do next. In our first conversation, she admitted she was lost. I started coaching Lisa and naturally started with helping her define her values. Some of them were . . .

Animals = sense of peace

Shopping = exploring

Designing = my own product that makes me happy

Friends/people = bonding time

Party planning = putting the whole thing together

Being appreciated = I made someone feel good

Exercising outdoors = therapeutic

Working with people = restoring someone's self-confidence

Cleaning = sense of accomplishment

Purpose/passion = happiness and joy for myself and others

Those may seem like a random list as you read them, but the more we talked, three values popped out:

Friends/people = bonding time

Working with people = restoring someone's self-confidence

Passion/purpose = happiness and joy for myself and others

From there Lisa realized that one of her most important values was helping others. Even in her previous roles, she was the one to comfort patients, letting them know that everything would be all right whether it was their medical procedure or their bill. Lisa had pushed away the thought of using her psychology degree because she didn't want to be a traditional psychologist, but she didn't realize she could use it in other roles that were aligned with her values.

She then looked through the Bureau of Labor Statistics list and found numerous roles that interested her and narrowed the list to five possibilities:

→ Child psychologist

→ Organizational psychologist
→ Consumer psychologist

→ Police psychologist

→ Life coach

The only one Lisa knew existed before looking at the BLS list was the first one.

To understand each career a little more, I gave her homework to Google all of them individually to learn more about them, including additional schooling or skills needed, and to reflect on what excited her about what she found. She learned, for example, that a child psychologist is a sub-specialty of clinical psychology. She would need to get her master's and PhD and do a one-year internship before completing her PhD. To get licensed, she would need to practice an additional year under supervision. When she took her pulse after reading about it, she reported, "I don't believe I have enough excitement to move forward on this one."

When Lisa researched "organizational psychologist," she learned she would likely need a master's or doctorate degree and that the growth rate for this career is about 35% over the next decade. She learned about its core focus on training and development, compensation and reward systems, and organizational change. Then she remembered that this was the career she had picked when she was getting her bachelor's but had dismissed it at the time because it required a master's and she was already overwhelmed just finishing her BA. As Lisa explored it now, years later, she reported remembering why she was so excited about it. "I feel like I would be making a difference in employees' lives and the positions I could get are so varied. I could work for different kinds of companies that focus on things I am passionate about such as animals, design, and fashion."

Once you narrow down your list and find roles that appear interesting, dig in and research the job title using the word "job." For example, I found a job called "Chocolate taster." I love chocolate so I Googled "chocolate taster jobs" and found an article titled "Cadbury Is Hiring a Chocolate Taster and the Only Qualification Is 'A Passion for Confectionary.'"[2] I mean, wow! It sounded fascinating just by the headline! When I read the story, I learned it was part-time. I found another article on *Reader's Digest*'s website titled, "5 Secrets about Being a Professional Chocolate Taster,"[3] which was written by Oretta Gianjorio, an actual chocolate taster for Mars Chocolate-UC Davis Chocolate Panel. All of this helped to explain the exact nature of the job. It turned out to sound much less glamorous or exciting to me, but others may be enticed to learn more.

Another path of research is actual job descriptions (LinkedIn is a good source). Start with a job title at the level of vice president (VP) or senior vice president (SVP). By looking at the highest job in the field, you can learn all the possible types of work within that category. If you Google the job title and the word "job," you may only find entry-level positions, which will have mostly simple tasks. You may need to start in that lower level, but this exercise is about learning what the overall career is about, not just pieces of it. The VP or SVP descriptions will show you the trajectory of that career.

Talk to People

Once you have a basic understanding about which career seems interesting and what it will entail, you are ready to ask for "meet and greets" with people who know about or work in that field. Start by reaching out to those you know or someone who knows someone. You have friends. They have friends. Those friends have friends. You have a wide network of people who probably know someone in the field you are interested in. Ask one of them to email or personally introduce you to the person you want to talk with. If an introduction is made via email, immediately respond and ask what time works best for them to chat. I am always amazed when someone is interested in a specific career and a colleague of mine agrees to make contact and then the person looking to change careers doesn't follow up. Even if you've changed your mind or remain unsure, respond and/or take the call. You never know what you may learn!

If you don't know someone in the prospective career, I have found that even strangers will give 15 minutes of their time for you to pick their brains. Just ask Lisa. She reached out to professionals in both life coaching and organizational psychology and learned from coaches that those jobs aren't as stable as she thought. They require constant marketing to find new clients. She realized in talking to them that she had a new value—stability! She wanted to have a reliable job and a title that went with it. That helped her eliminate independent coaching as an option. She used her network and found numerous professionals in organizational psychology to talk to, and every conversation confirmed her belief that this was the right choice. She not only learned about the career itself; she also asked managers what they looked for in hiring so she'd know what practicums and internships to focus on. She reported that each conversation was helpful and the people were incredibly generous with their time and knowledge.

Of that, I had no doubt. People love to talk about themselves. Lisa did use her network to get introductions to people in the fields she wanted to learn about but found plenty of strangers to talk with. Without a friend's introduction, reach out to someone you don't know with an email on social media such as LinkedIn, Facebook, and Instagram through their messenger apps. Do some research first and see if you can find a connection (e.g., alumnus of the same college or have mutual friends). Without a connection, a simple message can look like this:

Dear [Contact Name],

Your long career in marketing has given you vast knowledge about the field in every aspect, from the agency side to B2B and B2C companies. I am looking to transition to a new career in marketing and I'm looking for some advice. I'm hoping you can make yourself available for 15 minutes either on the phone or in person at your convenience to answer some questions about marketing and your own career trajectory in the field. I appreciate your time and hope you can provide your availability to speak.

Best,

[your name]

If you have a college connection or you worked with that person in the past, make sure you say that in the first line: "I'm not sure if you remember me, but we worked together at [company name]," or "I'm an alumnus of Georgetown University and I noticed you work in [specific] field." Yes, it's that simple!

Further, if your values have already identified the industry you want to work in (e.g., medical, technology, financial, entertainment), reach out to recruiters in that specific field through LinkedIn. You might be thinking, *Why would a recruiter talk to me?* Not all will. Some won't even respond to your request. But some will if you reach out in a way that is approachable and doesn't beg for a job:

Hi [Contact Name],

I am looking to transition to a new career, but I have been having trouble determining where my skills could bring the greatest value to a company. I would love to pick your brain for 15 minutes about how I may be able to transfer my skills effectively. I have attached my resume for background and hope you can provide your availability to speak.

Best,

[your name]

Again, it's really that simple, but **DO NOT** pitch yourself for a job on these calls, even if you see one that interests you at the company where the recruiter works. You can ask what skills they look for in that type of role but don't sell yourself in any way because that's not the intent of your call. If the conversation goes well, the recruiter may suggest that you reach out if you see anything on the company career site. When you write a thank-you note (and yes, you should write one), that's the time to say you noticed a specific role (if indeed you did) and how you think your skills relate to that role. Meet and greets are designed to learn about a field and build a relationship with the person willing to take your call. If that leads to something more, all the better, but never push it!

I gave this advice to Annie, who was graduating college in six months with numerous marketing internships on her resume but still not convinced she wanted to work in marketing. She emailed and connected to dozens of people over the course of her last year of school targeting different areas of marketing interest (communications, PR, brand, partner, and product marketing). Before she made these calls, she put together a fantastic roadmap for these types of reach-outs and has shared what worked with me. I have also added some suggestions of my own:

→ **Say hello!** Ask casually how his/her day is going and thank the interviewee for taking time to talk to you.

→ **Briefly introduce yourself, why you reached out.** Are you interested in knowing more about the industry/the interviewee's career path? Also, explain how you found him/her. Was it random? Did you have something in common such as graduating from the same college or working at a former workplace you interned or volunteered at?

→ **If the conversation starts flowing organically, stay in the moment without a specific agenda.** Reminder: You are trying to make a "connection" and build a relationship. Some discussions will be a "one and done" and some will lead to long-term mentorship or advice.

→ **Consider asking the interviewee if he/she has any questions *for you* before starting with your own questions.** This step isn't necessary but may be useful if there is any "suspicion" as to why you have so many questions. Just be honest; you are researching the skills needed to be successful in the field and seeking advice for your own trajectory by learning from their success.

→ **Ask questions.** Have a list of potential questions but don't ask them all because it's best to keep the conversation organic and flowing. Examples include:

  ◆ What was your journey like from graduating college to where you are now?

  ◆ My skills include (fill in the blank), and I'm hoping you can help me understand how to best combine them to bring the greatest value to a company.

  ◆ What hard and soft skills do you look for when hiring someone in your field?

- Is there one specific skill that is a "must have" in your field?
- What kinds of decisions do you make on a daily, weekly, or monthly basis?
- What is it about (insert profession) that excites you the most?
- What is the most challenging part of your job?
- What is one thing about this career that people from the outside don't know?
- What skills do you think were necessary to move up in your career?
- If talking to a people manager: What do you look for when hiring someone on your team?
- How have you seen your field change in the time you've been in it?
- I'm trying to wrap my head around "workplace culture." Have you noticed different cultures in the various jobs you've had, and can you describe them?
- In your entire career, is there a company culture you liked the best and why?
- What advice do you have for someone like me trying to break into this field?
- What is the best piece of advice you received from a former mentor?
- Is there something you know now that you wish your younger self knew then?

After your conversation, don't forget to send a thank-you note via email. A mailed note is fine if you don't have an email address. Someone just took precious time out of their day to give you advice. You are thanking them for their time and expertise. Write that you will keep in touch as you progress in transferring to a new career, and then do just that. Keep in touch.

Once you've spoken to a person about their career, you've just made a new connection and laid the foundation to build a relationship. Don't lose the connection or torpedo the relationship by disappearing. Also, don't annoy the connection by reaching out every week. There is a rhythm to keeping in touch that is like an art form. I suggest reaching out when something significant happens, such as when you . . .

→ settle on the career of your choice and starting to apply for jobs in the field.

→ finish and pass a certification exam.

→ finish some courses in the field.

→ go back to school to get more experience in a field (shows you are dedicated).

→ have been keeping in touch with your contact for a while and notice he/she is connected to the hiring manager or someone at the hiring company for a position.

→ are visiting the town your contact is in and you'd love to bring him/her a cup of coffee and visit for 30 minutes. (Be prepared with more questions!)

→ want to wish the contact a happy holiday or a great summer.

→ graduate from college and are on the job hunt.

→ just want to give an update (every six months or so).

→ are on your final interview for a position and would like any final advice.

→ accept a new role. Always circle back with your contacts once you've found a new position so they know where you are and what you are doing.

With the right cadence, a contact may become a mentor or even your boss someday. At the very least, they become a professional relationship. It is therefore important to maintain communication but not become a burden or a pest: "Hey, just thought I'd check to see if you are you working on anything interesting?" Remember, this is a professional contact, not a friend. They may be kind and generous with their time, but they aren't sharing their daily lives with you. It's like having a coach. Coaches don't mingle their own lives with those of their clients. The focus is on the client. The same goes for the person who is changing careers or looking for their first job. The focus is on you and that is okay!

So when you reach out to a contact, it should only be about asking for advice, providing an update, or, if you've built a longer-standing relationship over time, you can ask for your colleague to refer you to a company that has a role you found. Notice I said, "A role you found." My favorite example of the wrong way to stay in touch is when someone sends a contact their updated resume and asks if they've "heard of any jobs" out there. Most people aren't in the job market or in the job market at your level. By asking contacts to let you know if they've "heard about any openings," you are implying that they do your job search for you. Once you've built a solid relationship and your contact believes you could be a solid contributor to a team, he/she will automatically keep you in mind if they hear about an opportunity that is right for you.

If there is a position at your contact's company and you've built a rapport, ask if they have any information on the role beyond the job description or whether the role reports to your contact. If they feel comfortable with you, he/she may offer to refer you the role without you even asking. If it's at another company, ask your contact if they know anything about that other company—the leadership, the culture, and/or the role itself.

Stop!

Okay, now stop. Take your pulse (not literally, figuratively). How are you feeling? Are you overwhelmed with what it takes to change careers or find your first job? If yes, reread the parts in Chapter 1 on fear. Lisa felt overwhelmed at first and described herself as feeling "down" and "hopeless" because she didn't know how to go forward. But once she started talking to people, I could hear the excitement in her emails and voice when we spoke about what she was learning. When I asked her if she was still feeling confident that this was the right path, her answer was clear. "At first I thought I'd have to take a crappy job and hope to work myself up. Now I know what I want to do and I'm super excited for the future. This process has opened up a whole new world for me. My husband is excited about it. My mom is excited about it. I feel really good and energized." That is the feeling you are looking for—excitement about your future.

Don't Give Up

It may take dozens of phone calls in a single field to learn it's not the right one for you, but it can only take one phone call to set your trajectory. When I was looking for a new career, I had no idea what I wanted to do and I wasn't sure if my skills were transferable. In fact, I could count on one hand the number of people in the entire country who did exactly what I did.

I did the steps above and I narrowed down my choices to public relations or some type of communications like corporate communications or internal communications because I loved writing and formulating messages and giving advice on how to position an issue. My second thought was working as a legislative assistant—someone who drafts and edits state or federal legislation including bills or rules and who helps propose and research ideas for legislation. I know that's an odd combination, but I majored in political communication in college and part of my most recent position dealt with immigration: moving production crews around the world and bringing in talent for shows like the *MTV Movie Awards* and Nickelodeon's *Kids' Choice Awards*. In fact, I became so interested in immigration that by the time I left, I was giving advice internally without outside counsel help. I also worked with our internal lobbyists to get language in the "Gang of 8" immigration bill (known as the Border Security, Economic Opportunity, and Immigration Modernization Act of 2013), which allowed reality show participants to perform on unscripted television on a visitor's visa when not part of a competition show (like *Tosh.0*). I loved working on that project even though the bill never made it to law.

So, I started reaching out to people in those fields. As expected, some people didn't return my email or LinkedIn messages. Some said they were too busy to talk to me. After a woman on LinkedIn accepted my request to connect, I emailed her a nice invitation to speak for 15 minutes about what she does as a legislative aid. She wrote back immediately. "I knew if I connected to you it would be a risk that you would want something and I'm running for a city council seat right now and don't have time to talk." I thought, hmmm, I won't be voting for you! Eventually, at least one person in both the public relations/communications and legislative assistant fields agreed to talk to me. Unfortunately, both conversations left me more lost than ever and feeling that neither career was a perfect fit. The PR-type roles seemed boring. I couldn't imagine writing press releases or hounding the press all day for coverage and determining my success based on how many "impressions" each story received. The legislative assistant role was overwrought with politics. Surprise! I knew I'd get frustrated if something never moved forward. I would also have had to move to Sacramento (the capital of California) or D.C.

I decided to reach out to recruiters. On LinkedIn, I happened upon one recruiter from eBay (now at LinkedIn) who wrote on his profile, "If you need career advice, happy to give it!" Great, I thought, and I wrote him a simple LinkedIn message:

Hi Nathan,

I saw on your LinkedIn Profile that you would be willing to give career advice. I am looking to transition to a new career, but I have been having trouble determining where my skills could be most effective in a company. I would love to hear your perspective about how I may be able to transfer my skills. I know your time is valuable and would only need about 15 minutes.

Best,

Marlo

Note that I mentioned how my skills could be most effective *to a company*. I learned early in my career that it's not all about me. When looking for a new job, it's about finding a hole that needs to be filled *and* filling it with your skills. Most people are looking through the lens of "What do I want to do?" That's a great place to start, but you will have to translate how your skills are transferrable and will directly benefit that company. In writing the message the way I did, I wanted to make sure the recruiter knew I was looking for the right fit, not just any new job. He was nice enough to write back and we scheduled a call at his first available time, six weeks later, the Wednesday before Thanksgiving, 2016. Little did I know this would be the single most important and informative call I had initiated and the catalyst for my career transition.

I started the conversation by thanking him for his time; I knew it was valuable and he didn't have to take a call from a random stranger. I explained that I thought he might be able to help me since he'd been a recruiter at numerous companies in numerous fields. I didn't assume he had looked at my LinkedIn profile, so I explained that the reason I reached out was because I had these unique and diverse skills, had explored a number of fields such as PR/Communications and Government Affairs, and knew they weren't for me. I explained my broad background (lawyer mind, analytical skills, immigration and risk expertise, TV reporting, communication) and that I didn't know what to do with it all.

He asked me a few questions about what I loved about my current job. I had my values list in front of me and explained that I really enjoyed coaching, mentoring, advising, solving problems, and working cross-functionally. I loved being a part of a company that felt relevant.

He said, "It sounds like you may like being an HR business partner." I politely explained that I'd thought of HR but wasn't an employment lawyer, had little expertise in that field, and wasn't interested in doing typical HR work like harassment trainings and investigations or processing leaves of absence. He said, "No, it's not tactical like helping people file for leaves of absence. It's strategic, working alongside leadership to help the business grow through talent and determining what people skills are needed to do that." He also explained that it's working with senior executives on organizational effectiveness and organizational design. Huh, I thought. I had only known HR people to be generalists. I had never met a strategic HR person in my nearly 20 years of working and in fact had no direct interaction with HR in any of my jobs—except when I was fired. Clearly, my perception was not the reality. He suggested doing some research and look only for HR Business Partner positions that had the word "coaching" in the job description. I thanked him for his time and promptly started researching.

It didn't take long to realize that there are many jobs titled "HR Business Partner" and none of them are the same. Some were tactical as I'd assumed: administering benefits and compensation. Some were focused on creating learning and development programs. Some were more operations based. And some were very strategic, as Nathan had explained. I never realized that one job could have so many variations. I looked at each description, the size of the company, the industry the company was in, and so on. I couldn't find a pattern because each company viewed the HR function differently, though I did find the strategic HR Business Partner roles mostly in tech companies.

He was also right that the jobs I most resonated with had the word "coach" in them. I called a colleague who had left Viacom not long before and was now the "chief people officer" at a start-up tech company. She filled me in about how the HR Business Partner role works inside companies. I also mentioned my information quest to a friend who told me that a former sorority sister of ours was a successful executive business coach and could be a great lead. I called her and she explained that coaching is not mentoring but a more formal way of helping someone realize their potential. So far, everything sounded great. Now I just needed to figure out how to show that my skills were transferrable.

Repeat this chapter over and over until you have landed on a potential career (or two) that you want to pursue. You may decide on one, but as you learn more about it, you may discover that it sounded much better than it is in real practice. Being a lawyer is a great example. Some people love practicing law, but many realize in their first law job, it's not what they thought. Being a lawyer is mostly about writing, positioning, influencing, interpreting, and negotiating. That means sitting behind a desk and reading and writing most of the day. Unless a lawyer pursues civil litigation or criminal law as a practice area, he/she may never perform in front of a jury. Most attorneys push paper, not the exciting dramas you see on TV.

Alternatively, you may hear about a career that sounds boring until you dig in and learn the nuances. I always thought HR was about processing leaves of absence and hiring and firing people. I had no idea how much fun it could be working behind the scenes, influencing senior leaders to be better leaders, communicators, and managers, and helping employees adapt to a change. So be like a detective trying to uncover clues—the good as well as the bad—to help you solve the case of the long-lost dream career.

Chapter 3 Summary

1. **Hard and soft skills:** Review your values to clarify hard and soft skills that help you fulfill those values.

2. **Determine "no" careers:** Figure out which careers you absolutely can't do even though they seem like obvious choices based on your skills.

3. **Find potential careers:** Look at the BLS website and other websites that list career positions in every field. Narrow down choices that excite you.

4. **Research careers:** Research all possible careers and look at job descriptions to further narrow down choices.

5. **Talk to people:** Set up phone or in-person "meet and greets" to gain more insight into careers you may not know about and then build relationships with people in those fields.

6. **Repeat:** If you did all the steps in this chapter and still have not landed on a career that excites you, do it again. You may have short-changed yourself in one of the steps or missed a career that is perfect for you.

CHAPTER

4

Experience Comes in Many Ways

"An investment in knowledge pays the best interest."
—Benjamin Franklin, founding father of the United States

Now that you've narrowed down your potential career choices, it's time to get real. Do you need additional education? Do you need specific skills like multi-language fluency? Do you need a certification? Even if you don't need anything else to do the job you've chosen, how do you show potential employers you are serious about this new or first career?

Determine Needed Job Skills and Experience

Many jobs don't require a higher degree such as in law or for practicing medicine. Where no advanced education is required, it is up to you to determine what undergraduate degree, master's degree, or certification you may need. The four easiest places to find answers are LinkedIn profiles, job descriptions, meet and greets, and Google.

> **Tip #4: Research the types of degrees, certifications, languages, and/or experience you will need or should have for the new career.**

1. LinkedIn profiles: These are great sources of information for both introductions and learning about different career paths. Look for patterns. Does everyone have an MBA or a higher degree or a bachelor's with a specific major? If you want to work in an international job, what kind of fluency shows up in these profiles? When looking at experience, do you see the use of data? And if so, which data sets are most prominent in a particular field? Do you see specific kinds of projects? Repetitive words? LinkedIn profiles are great for figuring out the true crux of a specific job and the types of skills, degree, or certification needed to be successful.

2. Job Descriptions: Job descriptions are also full of information. Research VP and SVP roles as well as lower-level positions in your chosen career to identify patterns of experience and formal education. Look at "job requirements," "desired qualifications," and language skills needed. "Required" technically means "necessary," but you'd be surprised at how many requirements aren't really required. For example, there was a "required 30% travel" for my HR job. I was really concerned about being on the road and away from my kids. That said, I traveled twice in the first year. So, don't dismiss a job just because there's a requirement you don't have or one that makes you feel uneasy unless it's an obvious reach such as working in France with fluency in French.

"Desired" or "preferred" qualifications means a recruiter is looking for someone with a certain degree or experience and will give such resumes a closer look, but it's not a deal breaker if you don't have them.

For a general sense of what the role requires, look for repetitive words or job duties. For example, in the strategic HR roles I sought out, I saw "coach" on multiple lines. I had coached my previous direct reports and some cross-functional colleagues, but I thought there may be more to this "coaching" thing, so I started researching "executive coach" and "certification." I learned that there were lots of certification courses, but I couldn't figure out if I definitely needed to take them and, if so, which ones. So . . .

3. Meet and Greets: Asking the right questions in meet and greets about necessary education or certifications will also help you determine if you have—or can get—all the requirements. During my transition, I again called on some of my previous contacts and talked to some new ones as well. In general, they didn't think getting certified in coaching was absolutely necessary, but we also agreed that it would be hard to show I had coaching experience based on my current role. That meant getting certified *was* necessary. Huh? Let me explain.

It probably isn't necessary for someone with 20 years of HR experience behind them because they hopefully learned how to coach organically. But someone with no such experience needs to show that they know what coaching really means and can show some relevant experience in it. I knew how to manage, mentor, and inspire, which I thought translated to "coach," but I realized from researching certification programs and subsequently taking courses with the Co-Active Training Institute that coaching is a highly structured discipline. Getting a coaching certification would not only give me the tools I needed to be a successful coach, it would prove to a prospective employer I had the right experience.

Lisa learned the same thing when talking to people in Industrial/Organizational Psychology. Some people thought she only needed a bachelor's degree, but they had been working in the field for 20+ years and had built up their credibility. If she didn't want to start at the bottom, she would need to get her master's as well as a bevy of internships and a practicum—efforts she had to evaluate whether she was willing to take to move into the field.

4. Google: Try different combinations such as "career name + credential" or "education + position" or "career name + certification." Most careers don't need an advanced degree or a specific credential but do have certification programs. For example, HR has different certifications including PHR (Professional Human Resources), SPHR (Senior Professional Human Resources), and GPHR (Global Professional Human Resources). The Society for Human Resource Management (SHRM) also has comparable certifications such as the SHRM-CP (Certified Professional) and SHRM-SCP (Senior Certified Professional). While they may be "desired" or "preferred," none of them are *required* to work in HR. And neither company's certifications are more prestigious than the other. Also, colleges and universities offer master's programs as well as certificates in human resources but these, too, are not required to work in the field. So why bother?

The biggest benefit of working toward a certification or an advanced degree in your area of interest is that you can learn about the field both tactically and philosophically. You may also end up doing projects while earning a degree, which can be used on your resume as experience. Finally, once you have some knowledge about a field or a specific position, you will have more to talk about during meet and greets. For example, if someone in HR asks you, "Can you give me an example where change management went really well and an example where it went really poorly?" you will probably have a good answer!

Another Google search could focus on skills such as, "Skills needed to be a great data analyst." A plethora of results will pop up, but some basic skills are Microsoft Excel, SQL, R or Python, Data Visualization, and Machine Learning. A few soft skills might include presentation skills, critical thinking, and distilling large amounts of information into actionable insights. By knowing what skills are needed, you can determine what courses are available to learn them and whether you can gain practical experience in those skills in your current job.

How many of these skills do you need when transitioning careers? As many as possible. When you are transitioning, you can't just say, "Sure, I can do that! I'm great and brilliant!" Of course, you are! But how do you prove it? By showing that you are serious about this transition through the steps you've taken to get there: your researching the field, talking to people, making time to obtain a degree or certification, taking internships or volunteer opportunities. Once you show dedication to the transition, it's easier to influence how the rest of your skills will transfer to the new career. This is especially true if you took some time off work and are now trying to re-enter the workforce. Taking a few courses will show you've kept your skills fresh while learning new ones. Of course, the pursuit of courses, certifications, or higher degrees will require some resources.

Finances

Look for inexpensive ways to gain the necessary knowledge or experience. If you want to go back to school, look for colleges that offer reduced or even free tuition. For example, want to become a software engineer and only pay tuition if you get a job? Check out Holberton School: https://www.holbertonschool.com and Make School https://www.makeschool.com/. Other places include your local community college or local university "extension" classes for those not enrolled as full-time students. UCLA https://www.uclaextension.edu/ has hundreds of such courses and some are online. *U.S. News & World Report* found that some schools will offer free tuition if you give back afterwards or come from certain states or socio-economic backgrounds.[1] For example, Alice Lloyd College offers free-tuition education for full-time students from the counties that surround the Central Appalachian service area. Some schools offer free tuition in exchange for working on campus.

If a full-time commitment isn't an option or you just want to take a few courses or get a certificate in a specific area, consider Coursera (www.coursera.com), which is a hot site for free courses. A *Forbes* article touts Udemy.com, an online resource for courses created by content creators in 50 languages.[2] Codecademy.com is free and will teach you how to code in different programming languages for careers in data science, web programming, and software engineering. Stanford Online also offers free courses and certificates in numerous areas including Project Management, Predictive Modeling, Clean Energy, Mathematics, and Engineering. Finally, consider investing in a membership to LinkedIn Learning www.linkedinlearning.com/learning. There you can learn how to master both hard skills from Excel to SQL and soft skills from "How to Be an Inclusive Leader" to "Creating a High-Performance Culture."

Time

As you learn what additional education or experience you may need to launch into your new career, you will want to determine a realistic timeline to transition. Were you just terminated from a job with no severance or savings? Were you terminated months ago but your severance is running out? If your livelihood is at stake or you have other priorities such as young children or an ill parent, it may take longer to make a career transition. Set expectations for yourself so you don't get frustrated about how long it may take to set yourself up for success. I had to do that after I was terminated as a TV news reporter in Dayton, Ohio.

I loved journalism, especially the fast pace, meeting new people every day, and digging up and telling a great story. But I was drained from a lack of leadership and the fact that reporters had no power in the hierarchy of TV news to make any decisions. I can't tell you how many nights I stood in front of a dark building during the 11 p.m. news to report on a meeting that ended before 7. We also worked on holidays and weekends. I knew I wanted to change careers, but I also had to support myself. When my employment ended (remember I was fired!), I was paid out on my contract so I had a mere six weeks before the rent money ran out.

This was 1996 and the internet was just starting to become more commercial and popular. Google and LinkedIn didn't yet exist, though, so I didn't have some of the options you are reading about in this book. After talking to my parents and friends, I decided that the most obvious career transition would be into public relations or some kind of communications field. TV news, while grueling, *was* exciting. I was "in the field" or "on the road" meeting new people and covering different stories every day. It was going to take time to find the right career that would give me the same excitement, and sitting behind a desk writing press releases wasn't it. That's when I knew I had to get back into TV news and stabilize my journalism career while figuring out how to leverage my experience into another field.

So, I accepted a full-time job in Oklahoma City as a consumer investigative reporter at KWTV News 9, which felt like a step up from general assignment reporter. But I never again wanted to be in a job that didn't have transition potential to a new career, so I immediately started working on a backup plan.

I always thought that law was interesting and within months of arriving in Oklahoma, I applied to night law school at Oklahoma City University. I was fairly sure I didn't want to practice law, but I loved to learn and wanted something I could use if I was unemployed again. I started night law school less than a year later and, three and a half years later, I had a law degree!

Law school fit my schedule, but of course it wasn't easy. In fact, changing careers is never easy, and it may take multiple years to gain the right skill set or the degree you need to make the change, especially if you're working full-time, have kids, or dealing with other obligations. That's okay! When I decided to go to law school, I had a demanding, full-time reporter job, but I was motivated and willing to be patient. My goal was too important to give up on. If you are willing to commit and aware of the sacrifices you might have to make—and for those of you with a job, blessed with a supportive employer—your chances of success will be high.

Employer Support

Most employers don't want to lose an exceptional employee. If the degree or certification you are hoping to achieve aligns with your current role, most employers will be on board. Even if your motivation is to move into a new career, determine if those types of jobs exist at your current company. Marketing, HR, legal, finance, business development, and others exist in many companies. Ask for a "stretch assignment" in another group if it exists to gain experience.

One of my former employees on the Production Risk Team at Viacom was getting an MBA with a specialty in data science. While part of our job was to analyze background checks, psych exams, and medical exams to determine the level of risk for reality show candidates, it didn't rise to the level of data science. To support her degree work, I gave her as many analytic projects as I could so she could gain some practical experience, but I could tell she was frustrated and her work was starting to falter.

After a few months of watching her go through the motions of her job but clearly lacking passion for it, I sat her down and asked her softly, "What's going on?" She admitted that she just wanted to be like everyone else in her class, interning and learning from brilliant data scientists, but she couldn't leave her day job because she supported her family. She felt stuck. She finally knew what she wanted to do but thought this degree would be a waste of time without practical experience. I listened and asked her what her ideal job would be when she graduated. She said working as a data scientist in a media company. I mentioned she probably missed the deadline to interview for paid summer internships, so I said I would help her get one at our company. I offered to call the head of our data science team (whom I didn't know) to see if they'd be interested in interviewing my employee for an internship. They had already hired all the interns they had budget to hire for the summer, so I made it easy by saying I'd make her available full-time for six weeks while drawing a salary from my budget, not theirs. She interviewed and they offered her the position.

On the day she left, I walked into her office and declared my intention with these exact words: "Don't come back." I told her there were numerous openings in that department (listed on the company's jobs page) and my expectation was that she would fight for one of those roles by completing a stellar internship. She thanked me and I didn't hear another word.

About halfway through her internship, two managers in the data science department offered her their open positions. After much debate, she accepted one of them and honed her skills. Find your champion—someone who will help you get the experience you need to move to a role that fulfills your values. If you find that support from your manager, make sure you keep excelling in your current role.

Unfortunately, not every manager or company will be willing or is able to give an employee the same kind of opportunity. Even though my boss knew I was working on my certification in executive coaching and that I wanted to learn more about organizational design, I got little support. My manager was adamant in telling me, "People spend their entire careers in those areas. There will no opportunity for you to learn them in your present role." So I coached at night and on weekends and found HR leaders outside my company who described how they approached organizational design.

If you can't find opportunities at your current employer to gain some of the skills needed for a new career, consider volunteering at night or on weekends with a nonprofit—maybe your kids' school or your religious place of worship. Ask a friend in the field if you can shadow one of their projects or meet to discuss steps on something they are working on. Just don't let your outside activities affect your current work performance.

Once you've gained the knowledge and experience to move into the new career, and you want to do it at your current company, your boss won't support you if you aren't already an exceptional employee. "Showing up well" means having a good attitude, doing your job, and going above and beyond in your current role. If you let your work slack because you think you'll be gone in a few months, your boss may conclude that they'd be "moving a problem around." They may also be in the process of terminating your employment due to a lack of performance in your current role. This is not the way to approach your transition. In a few chapters, you will read about "backdoor references" and how those can affect your ability to gain employment elsewhere in a new field.

So even if you've mentally moved on from your current role, show up well every day and perform at your best. Use every opportunity to learn and grow, especially in soft skills because those are universal and needed for success in every job.

After being told there was no way to advance my skills in my current role or in a different role at my company, I continued to perform at an exceptional level and took the time to set myself up for success. That meant three months of studying at night and on weekends to prepare for the SPHR and GPHR certification exams and nearly a year to get certified in executive coaching. A year! I also took all my continuing legal education classes to keep my bar license after I changed careers in case it didn't work out and so I wouldn't be worried. I took online courses on soft skills through my company's learning portal and read a few books such as *The Start-Up of You* by Reid Hoffman and *The First 90 Days* to jazz me up about a new role.

You don't need to be an overachiever. Take your time to gain the core skills, knowledge, and education you need to make the move. The more certifications, degrees, classes, and experience you can show, the more likely you'll convince a hiring manager that you are working to truly understand the substance of a field and how it is practiced in the workplace. Patience is critical when you are investing in you.

Chapter 4 Summary

1. **Determine needed skills and experience:** Research degrees, certifications, and experience needed for the new career through reviewing LinkedIn profiles and job descriptions, taking meet and greets, and googling positions and skills.

2. **Finances:** Determine what it will cost to get those skills and experiences and/or alternative ways to obtain them.

3. **Determine time frame:** Based on your needs and situation, identify a realistic time frame to gain the right degrees, certifications, skills, and experience.

4. **Find supporters:** Look within your current company or outside your company to find supporters and mentors who will help you gain the experience. It may not be your current or former boss!

5

Learning the Lingo to Transfer Skills

"Learning a new language is becoming a member of the club—the community of speakers of that language."

—Frank Smith, contemporary psycholinguist

As we've been discussing, if you dream of working in a completely new career, you will need to figure out how to truly understand the field you've chosen and how your skills are directly applicable. The problem is that . . . you can't. Networking and job descriptions can help, but it's like adults without kids who comment on the parenting skills of friends with kids. They simply have no idea what it's like to be a parent. Babysitting is not parenting. Visiting friends who have kids is not parenting. Reading books will never explain what it's like on a day-to-day basis to be a parent. Once you do become a parent, you feel like you've joined a secret club of those who truly know what it's like, where you can talk about the ups and downs, rewards and challenges, like a pro. Moving into a new career is very similar. Since you haven't lived it yet, you will need to learn as much as you can about it and speak in ways that show you've done your homework and are serious about transitioning.

Tip #5: Learn the lingo to understand your chosen field and hone your message.

Learning the Lingo through Conversations

In 2016, LeEco was a tech darling. The company had just taken over a large campus in San Jose and was in the news daily for its offer to acquire Vizio. I connected with the VP of People Operations on LinkedIn and he was willing to meet with me. We talked for quite a while as he explained the difference between what he did compared to the HR Business Partner roles I was considering. This helped me further understand the nature and structure of Human Resources. He told me about the roles he had open on the operational side and thought it would be easier for me to transfer into one of those based on my experience. He was probably right, but as he described them, I knew they weren't right for me because I wanted to be business-facing and more strategic in my work with people. He also told me that operations roles aren't a natural gateway to HR Business Partner. By the end of our conversation, he offered to let me use his name to connect with the VP of HR Business Partners at LeEco. I emailed him and he agreed to a phone call.

This was a critical meeting. I was almost finished with my coaching courses and had just passed the HR certification exams. I had been researching and doing meets and greets for months and learning as much as I could about working in HR. I was ready to start applying for jobs. But since this was an informational meet and greet meeting only, I couldn't pitch myself directly for the open HR Business Partner roles at LeEco. My goal was to subtly convince him I was worthy of an in-person interview. While sitting in the parking lot of my final coaching class waiting for his call, I was thinking about how much I loved the coaching courses and helping people challenge themselves to overcome obstacles to be the best they can be. Finally, my phone rang. I answered, "Hi, this is Marlo." Then I blew it.

After the usual pleasantries, the first question he asked me was, "Why do you want to be an HR Business Partner?" I answered, "I want to help people." It was top of mind as I was about to enter my last coaching course in thirty minutes. He immediately said, "Wrong answer." He went on to explain that the main goal of HR Business Partners is to align people's skills with the goals of the business. Of course, I knew that from studying for my certifications and from previous conversations on organizational design, but I hadn't been using that as the crux of my message.

I knew in that moment I had lost any chance of interviewing in person for an HR Business Partner role at LeEco (even though it was a blessing; a week later, the China-based company started pulling out of San Jose). What felt like one of the worst meet and greets I ever had turned out to be one of the most helpful in teaching me how to use the right lingo to position myself for the role I wanted. From that day forward, I answered that same question more than a dozen times in language that was understood by HR leaders.

Connecting Skills

Once you understand the field you've chosen and the lingo used, it will be easier to connect how your skills from previous roles are directly applicable to those needed for the new role. When I wanted to transition into HR, I had more than a decade of TV news reporting experience and more than a decade of business risk experience. I had no actual experience *in* HR. Notice I said "in." I did have HR experience. Both of my previous jobs focused on people in different ways. The words underlined below connect my TV news experience with the world of HR.

My news jobs required me to <u>*influence*</u> people to talk with me on camera or provide information under difficult circumstances, such as after a loved one had passed away when I would knock on the door of a family who had just lost a child or a husband or a mother. I had less than three seconds to convince people to talk to me, hopefully on camera, or that door would slam in my face. That means I also had to be <u>authentic</u>. Because the news aired every night at set times, I was always working in a <u>fast-paced environment</u> with a hard deadline. If I wasn't successful, there would be a "hole" in the newscast. As an investigative reporter, I had to <u>research and source the truth</u> and <u>distill a lot of information</u> into a simplified story that could be understood. Finally, I had to have <u>on-air presence</u> when presenting stories to the public.

On the surface, it doesn't appear that my TV news work had anything to do with HR, but if you look at the skills needed in HR, there was plenty of relevance. For example, it's critical to <u>source the truth during an in-house investigation</u> to discover the root of a problem when two departments or two people aren't getting along and jeopardizing <u>company productivity</u>. Presenting live and on air provided me with <u>executive presence</u> and <u>presentation skills,</u> which I continue to use today, especially in front of the C-Suite. Finally, many companies think they are fast-paced, but nothing is faster than turning around a story every day for the 5 p.m. news when your photographer isn't available until 3, or breaking news happens at 4:30 and you need to go live with it in 30 minutes. HR requires someone who <u>can maintain executive presence under pressure, deal with uncomfortable conversations, influence in an authentic way,</u> and work at an <u>incredibly fast pace.</u> See how it all connects when you look at your previous work and role through the lens of the new role?

Working in "production risk" also focused on people—reality show participants. Every reality show needs certain people who "<u>fit</u>" in the overall cast to make it successful and <u>drive business</u> (aka viewership). Have you ever noticed that most shows have one person who can be edited to look "crazy?" Or the "smooth talker," the "maternal mom"? In reading thousands of reality participant psychological reports and background checks and then watching those personalities play out on set, I <u>understood all kinds of people on a deeper level.</u> I also had to evaluate how I thought each person would <u>perform under the pressure</u> of glaring lights and television cameras and whether they could cope after production and when the show aired. When the show went into production, I would deal with <u>crisis management</u> when people clashed in an unacceptable or dangerous way on set. At times, some of them regretted what they had said on camera and would threaten to harm themselves if a show aired. I had to intervene during or after production to ensure they and the rest of the cast and crew were safe, while <u>coaching TV producers and company executives</u> on what to do. Pull the show? Keep airing it? I had to use <u>exceptional judgment</u> to constantly <u>manage sensitive situations</u> while keeping productions moving forward, because if the production shut down or the network pulled the show, that could mean a loss of millions of dollars.

I have other examples from other positions and experiences, but you get the picture. With all those skills, it wasn't hard to connect them to HR Business Partner skills. HR recruiting is about hiring people who have the <u>right fit for the role both from a skills perspective and a culture perspective</u>. My management experience combined with my unique ability to understand people on a deeper level—how to <u>look at their skill sets</u> and where they could <u>stretch their skills</u>—would allow me to help <u>align those skills with business goals</u>. Also, I had an ability to <u>coach senior executives</u> on what would <u>positively (or negatively) impact their business</u>. A stretch? Sure, but still a connection of skills.

Using HR terminology to describe the work I did as a business leader outside of HR showed I was "doing" HR without actually "being" in HR. By connecting the two skill sets and learning the lingo, I was able to open doors. And that's the key—learning the right language will align your current career to your dream career and convince a hiring manager to see how you would bring a unique perspective to the role.

Bringing a Unique Perspective

Without insulting people who spent their entire career in HR, coming from outside HR gave me unique insights into the <u>people, pressures, and priorities</u> of a business. Experience you have gained in your current career, no matter how different from the one you want, will be applicable while giving you a fresh perspective on the new career. Please repeat this because it's so important: <u>Your experience from your current or previous roles will give you a fresh perspective on the new job</u>. Taking that perspective and using the lingo of the new career to describe your current experience will show a hiring manager that you'll bring something to the position that no other candidate has. That will be appealing to growth-minded hiring managers because most of them have been in their roles for a long time and are seeking fresh perspectives.

Ben is a perfect example of someone who had a career that seemingly wasn't applicable to any other. He was working on film and television sets in "physical asset management," in charge of all the props and making sure the sets were dressed (decorated) for each day's shoot. He was working crazy hours and wanted nothing more than to find a career that would allow him to be home for dinner with his young children. He also wanted stability. Once his assignment on a TV show or film finished, he had to fight for the next job, never knowing how long he'd be unemployed before landing the next gig. But set dressing? How is that applicable to any other career outside of film and TV production? He had some experience as an executive assistant to film producers and literary agents and some other project management experience, but there was no common thread through his decade of work experience.

At first he explored moving into production safety because he understood safety from a set dressing perspective and knew it was a field that lacked enough people for all the work. He knew some of the Occupational Safety & Health Administration (OSHA) requirements from being on sets and working with the safety directors, and had picked up enough lingo to keep an interview going. To shore up his knowledge, he completed some OSHA certification courses he knew he would need and to help him with additional lingo. Then he honed his message and unique perspective that his years on sets made him a better candidate than someone with OSHA knowledge, because he understood that set dynamics and his various roles and responsibilities would make it easy for him to influence a crew to comply with safety requirements.

As he started to interview for production safety roles at some of the largest studios, confident he could translate his current work to the new role and fulfill some of his values such as having a stable paycheck and being more independent, he knew that becoming a production safety executive wouldn't fulfill his most important value. He would still be working crazy hours and for weeks at a time, often traveling around the world, keeping him away from his young children. The closer he got to this new career, the more he realized the sacrifice he'd be making—a sacrifice that almost seemed worth it just to get out of the set dressing world, which was becoming intolerable.

As he was in the final rounds of interviews at a major studio for a production safety job, I heard about a role in content operations at Roku. I was told the technical aspects of the job could be learned and that the hiring manager needed someone who understood processes and people and had a great attitude. The role was hard to fill because most people didn't want to leave full-time employment for a full-time freelance job, which Ben was already doing. There was also very little on his resume that would scream he had the right skills or that he'd even be interested, but I mentioned the role to him anyway and he jumped at the opportunity. I was clear that while I could get him a screening interview, I could not get him the job. He had to do that by convincing the hiring manager he was a fit for the role, so I encouraged him to start by learning the lingo and finding a common thread in his current and former jobs to create a "unique perspective."

He went after it with vigor and quickly educated himself on the lingo of that type of work and the technology used, such as "title tracking," "file ingestion," "content delivery," "metadata," "technological systems," and "workflows." He couldn't actually say he worked with metadata or video distribution workflows because he hadn't, but he used lingo where appropriate to show he understood the concepts and the importance of the work he would be charged with doing.

Then he looked at his current experience through the lens of this opportunity. He connected the dots for the hiring manager (see the underlines on the lingo he used): He was part of a huge operation and knew how to organize massive amounts of inventory and information through inventory tracking software. He focused on his desire to work for a cutting-edge company, how he had to learn from scratch the technology he currently used, and that he had the skill to learn any new technology. He focused heavily on soft skills such as working under tight deadlines, solving problems as they arose, and adapting quickly to change because productions and direction were fluid. Most importantly, he gave no indication of being desperate to leave his current role, emphasizing instead how his experience laid the foundation for this new role.

His attitude and passion, combined with his ability to use the lingo of the job and connect the dots of multiple skill sets for the hiring manager, landed him the job, and he has since been converted to a staff employee.

No matter what you've done, you have skills. Look at them through the lens of the new career. You will be surprised at just how valuable they will be in the new career. You will bring something to the role that others will not—a unique perspective. Now you just need to find that perspective and hone your message.

Chapter 5 Summary

1. **Learn the lingo:** Research the language and concepts used in the new career and understand what they mean strategically and tactically.

2. **Connect skills:** Identify specific tasks in your current job that, if you simply changed the lingo, would directly relate to the role you want.

3. **Determine a unique perspective:** Determine how your experience from previous roles gives you a unique perspective for excelling at the new job.

4. **Hone your message:** Connect the dots on your resume and in interviews and adjust as you learn what is and isn't working in telling your story.

6

Recruiters Are the Gateway

"You can't knock on opportunity's door and not be ready."

—Bruno Mars, singer, songwriter, producer

You see a job that is perfect for you. You know you can do it. You apply online and attach your resume and cover letter and expect a call in the next week or so. Silence. You wait. Silence. And then, a few weeks or months later, you get the dreaded rejection email.

Unfortunately, we have decided not to proceed with your candidacy for the opening at Company. Hiring for this position is extremely competitive, and the candidate pool was very impressive. However, at this time, we have found a candidate who fulfills more requirements for the position.

Not even a call or a personal email. What happened? What happened is your resume probably wasn't even looked at. That's right.

IT. WASN'T. EVEN. LOOKED. AT.

Let that sink in.

First, who is looking at your resume? Recruiters. Hiring managers rarely look at resumes until recruiters flag the ones that are most relevant. That means your target audience is recruiters, which has also been called "Staffing" or "Talent Acquisition" leaders. For the purposes of this chapter, I will stick with recruiters.

It's important to understand the world of recruiters so you know who you are talking to and you understand how they work. There are two kinds of recruiters: Internal and External Recruiters. Each of those categories may include a specialized subcategory such as Executive Recruiters.

Tip #6: Think like a recruiter.

Types of Recruiters

Internal Recruiters

Internal Recruiters work inside a specific company and recruit for their employer (i.e., a recruiter who works at Google or Amazon and recruits only for that company). This type of recruiter has deep relationships with hiring managers and a deep understanding of the company culture because the recruiter works full-time inside the company. In many companies, this type of recruiter usually has a specialty such as General and Administrative (legal, HR, marketing, finance—any part of a company that isn't R&D) or R&D (engineering, data science, and other "technical"-type roles). In a start-up environment, Internal Recruiters may recruit for everything as there may only be one or two.

External Recruiters

External Recruiters have contracts with multiple companies to fill jobs. They are hired for many reasons such as when companies don't have Internal Recruiters or because a company is too small or Internal Recruiters have exhausted their search and the company needs an outside recruiter to target the right talent pool. External recruiters, either independent or with an agency, will sometimes specialize in the services they offer so they know the talent pool deeply in one or two industries. For example, The Winford Group, LLC, is known as one of the premier companies for recruiting business and legal affairs talent for studios, production companies, and entertainment companies, but it has also branched out into finance, marketing, creative, studio heads, and C-Suite.

Executive Recruiters can be internal or external. They seek out experienced and established executives to fill senior-level roles, in which the job is not always offered to the public. They may recruit for one industry or work across multiple industries. An example of an external executive recruiting agency would be Egon Zehnder or Spencer Stuart, which specialize in executive, CEO, and board advisory positions. Internal Executive recruiters may recruit for vice presidents or above as well. Jane Ashen Turkewitz, an independent recruiter at Hi-Touch Executive Search, specializes in recruiting high-level executives (director and above) for media and digital technology and has recently expanded into recruiting for cannabis companies.

Recruiters Don't Work for You

No matter what kind of recruiter you are talking to, they don't work for you; they work for companies. Alissa Block from The Winford Group says it best: "When I got into this business, I was a humanitarian and thought my mission was to help people find jobs. Hello, I cannot find people jobs! I feel horrible knowing and thinking this and horrible that I'm saying it out loud, but my job is not about finding people jobs. It's about finding the best talent for the client hiring me to do a search for them. It's capitalism."

All recruiters want to work with top candidates because placing one in a new role means they get paid. When a recruiter is engaging and encouraging and makes you feel special, they are selling you on the company and the job while determining if you are a good fit for the role and the company culture. That's why there's an old saying that goes, "You may never be treated as well by an employer as you were treated the first time you talked to a recruiter."

Some recruiters are lifelong relationship builders. Alissa says she has more than 15,000 people in her database. She's not alone. Jane Turkewitz started recruiting in digital in 1999 before digital was even a thing. Now, more than 20 years later, she has a huge database of senior-level people in both digital and emerging media. And since many executives she has placed in digital media jobs have been interested in moving into the cannabis space, she's been able to transfer into that space as well.

When she's working to fill a position, she may present two or three candidates to an employer. "I'm working with three candidates right now for one role. They all bring something different to the table and the client will need to make a decision. Two of those people will be disappointed, but I don't just disappear and dump them. They are now in my network and I will keep them in mind for future opportunities because they were professional throughout the entire process," says Jane.

That is also why you will want to build relationships and keep in touch with recruiters—they are seeking people daily for new openings. Also, some recruiters move jobs just like employees move jobs. They may not have represented a company you'd work for in the past, but you may be interested in the new one.

How Recruiters Work

Most recruiters don't have time to look at every resume in an Applicant Tracking System (ATS)—an online system for applying to an open position. Internal recruiters I spoke to said they usually look at the first 50 to 100 resumes in an ATS. If there is no viable talent in that pool of resumes, they will look at the next few dozen applicants. They rarely look through the entire applicant pool unless the pool is low or the company has full-time resume screeners, which is not that common. External recruiters I spoke to will start with their own databases first. If they don't have any viable candidates, they will reach out to their contacts or post and/or search on LinkedIn.

Every recruiter is working on filling numerous roles at one time, so they look at resumes of new candidates very quickly. "Look" means that a recruiter *scans* a resume for mere seconds. Literally. In a 2018 Eye Tracking Study,[1] the job search site Ladders.com revealed that recruiters screen a resume for an average of seven seconds. That's higher than a previous study in 2012 which said they screened resumes for six seconds. Whoopee. Bob Hancock, who has been recruiting for more than 20 years, currently manages a team of recruiters and says most positions receive at least 100 resumes and many have more than 500 applicants.

There is no chance of spending quality time on a resume. "If you can't project who you are and what experience you have so I can be intrigued to look at it longer than 10 seconds, then your resume isn't projecting your value."

Jane from Hi-Touch Executive Search agrees. For higher-level roles, she will spend up to 30 seconds on a resume. "I'm looking at their experience, how they progressed through their career. Did they experience growth in each company they worked for or in their transition to new jobs? Did they stay in the same industry or transition industries? What overall skill set do they have?"

Alissa from The Winford Group says she doesn't even post positions online because of all the resumes that don't match the job description. She reviews resumes from referrals for less than five seconds and from that says she can determine what brand name companies they worked for, what titles they've had, and whether their career trajectory was linear or took some twists and turns. "I honestly can't tell you if I have ever read a resume word for word. I scan straight down to the bottom and come back up."

I talked to dozens of recruiters and these three represent the consensus of most recruiters out there. Therefore, you have seconds to make an impression and show you have the right skills for the role, your career path and job move timeline makes sense, you have industry and/ or practical experience and/or transferable skills, and you are worthy of a phone call.

How Recruiters Find You

If recruiters don't already have a perfect candidate in mind from their network, some will post job descriptions or do a LinkedIn post explaining the opportunity and asking for referrals or applications. But not all perfect candidates are looking for a new role. So recruiters will also seek "passive" candidates who may not be actively looking to make a move but might be interested if they hear about a great opportunity. Recruiters mainly use LinkedIn while some pay for access to Indeed, Monster, and other job search sites for lower-level candidates. No matter the source, all recruiters do a Boolean search on LinkedIn using a string of hard skills that are critical to the job such as "SQL" or "Salesforce" or "revenue recognition." Their search will yield hundreds of potential candidates, some with the exact skills they are looking for and some with only a few. What you don't know is recruiters can also see three important things when searching LinkedIn:

1. **Candidates who've already applied.** Internal recruiters can identify from LinkedIn who has already applied to the job online through the company's Applicant Tracking System (ATS). If an External Recruiter posts the role, then they can see who applied to their posting. Internal recruiters will first start looking at candidates found in their Boolean search who have already applied to the role because those candidates have already shown a proactive interest and will be easier to recruit.

2. **A candidate's openness to new opportunities.** Recruiters can also see which LinkedIn profiles are set to "Open to New Opportunities." If you haven't checked your LinkedIn settings for a while, click on your picture (in the right corner next to notifications) and scroll down to Settings & Privacy. Make sure your Job Seeking Preferences are set in a way to be found along with your preference for location, industry, company size, and so on. This takes the guesswork out of what you want in your next role and allows recruiters to find you faster. Note: While LinkedIn tries to prevent people at your current employer from seeing if your LinkedIn profile is set to "Open to New Opportunities," it doesn't promise that someone won't find out. I checked with recruiters at my company when I was looking for a new role and they couldn't see that my profile setting was open. But if one of their friends sees it and tells them, it's possible your boss could find out as well.

3. **The likelihood of a candidate responding to an inquiry.**
Recruiters can determine who is more likely to respond to
their LinkedIn emails based on a candidate's previous emails
and responses to other inquiries. Recruiters can't see what
you wrote to other recruiters, but an algorithm will tell them
whether you are more likely to respond if recruiters reach
out. A former manager once told me, "Even if you are happy
in your job, take every call or at least return every email."
That's a lot of work if you are working full-time and happy in
your job. But there are reasons why you should take the time
to do this:

→ You never know when your company will downsize or change
direction and force you to look for a new opportunity.

→ You want the recruiter to know who you are even if the current job being pitched isn't the right role or the timing isn't
right today. As previously stated, Internal Recruiters change
jobs just like you! You never know where that recruiter will
be in a year or two or three. External recruiters may be relationship builders or have multiple roles they are trying to fill,
and you may be viable for another role at another company.

→ You can practice honing your message on every call.

Now you know how recruiters find you, but how do you make a
recruiter look at your resume or LinkedIn profile for more than seven
seconds and take the next step and call you?

Mastering the Applicant Tracking System

When you apply online, whether through LinkedIn, other job postings,
or directly on a company's website, you are applying to an applicant tracking system (ATS) if you aren't using email. It's the technology recruiters
use to keep track of applicants and move them through the interview and

hiring process. If you think of it as a place to apply for a single job, you are forgetting that every time you apply for a job at the same company, it stores your information.

So if you apply for more than one role at a company or you are pursuing more than one career option, you need to have multiple resumes. But keep in mind the ATS will show the recruiter all the jobs you've applied for and all the versions of your resume if you are tailoring it to a particular role. If those jobs are completely different, such as in finance or marketing, then it looks like you don't know what you want to do and are applying for anything and everything without a focus. That's a huge red flag for recruiters. Jane sees people sending resumes to every opening they find and multiple openings at the same company. "Candidates are making a big mistake by spraying and praying with their resumes. You must be strategic on what you go for because we get so many resumes. If you don't specify and customize your resume to the specs in the job description, you won't get any traction."

Therefore, if your experience translates to more than one role in different fields, don't apply for both of them at the same company. The exception to this is if you know someone at the company who believes your skills could be a great fit for multiple roles and is willing to champion you through the recruiting process.

In addition to recruiters, companies will use AI programs to search resumes for key words in the job description. This is another critical skill to master.

Make Transferable Skills Noticeable

Job seekers often read a job description, know they can do the job and have all the requisite experience, and yet never receive that call. Why? They probably didn't tailor their resume with the right key words. If you are transitioning careers, you have to work even harder to show you are the right person for a role you've never done before. Your resume and LinkedIn profile may be your first impression and needs to be discovered in a recruiter's Boolean search. Therefore, they must include at least 75% of the hard skills listed in the job description in clear, concise sentences.

For example:

Posted job description:

Company A is looking to hire a Staff Accountant to work in the SaaS-based industry, whose duties will be matching invoices to purchase orders/vouchers, processing Accounts Payable (A/P) and Accounts Receivable (A/R), and assisting in month-end.

Resume bullet point:

- Meticulous matching of invoices to purchase order/vouchers and processing accounts payable (A/P) and accounts receivable (A/R) in alignment with closing books at the month and year end.

Resume bullet point for an administrative assistant transitioning careers into finance but who has have never worked in finance:

- Submit purchase orders/vouchers and track accounts payable (A/P) and accounts receivable (A/R) against the department budget.

The administrative assistant doesn't say she *processes* accounts payables or accounts receivables but uses the key words from the job description to show that there is an understanding and has some experience with those concepts. By using "key words," it is more likely their LinkedIn profile will pop up in a Boolean search. Showing transferrable skills and using key words are critical to being found. An entire chapter (Chapter 9) is dedicated to highlighting transferrable skills.

Find a Connection to the Role or Company

Once you have applied online, don't expect a recruiter to review your resume unless you've made sure they see it. Recruiters don't review every resume in the ATS. Recruiters report they look at the first 50 resumes and if no one seems right for the role, then they will review the next 50 resumes. If you are applicant 125, your resume may never be viewed, even if it perfectly aligns to the role. That's why it's so important to contact a professional colleague in the company and the recruiter directly. If you can see the recruiter who posted the role on LinkedIn, apply through the link provided and then email the recruiter to tell them you applied to the role and why you are a perfect fit. Both Bob and Jane say they appreciate it if a candidate reaches out to them directly, as long as they reach out appropriately.

If you can't see which recruiter posted the position, start searching for a connection. On LinkedIn, see if you have mutual connections with others. If you don't have an obvious connection and you are applying for, say, a marketing job, do a LinkedIn or a Google search for "marketing, company name, recruiter name." If their profile says something like, "Staffing marketing roles at [company name]," you've probably found the right person. If you find recruiters at the company you are applying to but their profiles don't distinguish which specific area they recruit for, send them a LinkedIn message anyway because there's a good chance the one you found will pass along your information if your resume shows directly applicable skills.

If you can't find the recruiter, try to find someone at the company you know or a colleague who knows someone there. If it is a specific job within a field like "product marketing," do a LinkedIn search for "product marketing, company name" under LinkedIn People. You may find an SVP or VP who could be the hiring manager. Then see if you know anyone who knows that person. You can always send a LinkedIn message directly to the potential hiring manager in a specific area, but without a connection, that random communication may not elicit a response. Referrals are always the best way to be noticed by a recruiter and/or the hiring manager.

How to Approach a Recruiter

Approaching a recruiter can start a beautiful relationship or make a recruiter never want to talk to you again. Recruiters are usually filling more than a dozen roles at any one time. Your first email, resume, and/or LinkedIn profile must be perfectly aligned to the role you are applying for and it must be easy to read or you may never get a response. Look at your communication to a recruiter from their perspective. If they spent all day responding to every person who applied, no jobs would ever be filled! So only reach out if:

1. You have the right recruiter for your field. Reaching out to recruiters is fine if you know you are targeting the right recruiter for your field. If you find one who hasn't posted a role but works in the field in which you are seeking a position, reach out and introduce yourself. But if you are seeking a role in finance, don't reach out to a recruiter who only specializes in marketing (unless you acknowledge to the recruiter they are at the company you want to work for but realize they may not be the recruiter for this position).

When you do reach out, be extremely specific about why. Here's a great example:

Hi [recruiter name],

I'm reaching out because I am in the market for a new opportunity. Here is the type of role I'm seeking:

Position—Full-time employee. Not open to contract work.

Title—Director, Sr. Director, or VP of Brand or Consumer Marketing, B2C

Location—San Francisco Bay Area, no further southeast than Mountain View, no further north than San Francisco city proper. Open to full-time remote.

Industries—Technology, Software and Hardware, AI, Cybersecurity, Cryptocurrency, Med-tech. Not interested in ridesharing/self-driving auto companies.

Company—Prefer smaller company (under 5,000 employees) but open for right opportunity. Start-ups okay.

Compensation—Negotiable, minimum $200K total comp including equity. Must provide equity.

My resume is attached for your review. I look forward to hearing from you when you have a position where you think I could bring the most value.

Sincerely,

[your name]

Never reach out and say, "Hi, here's my resume if you have something," or "If you hear of anything, please let me know," or one of Jane's favorites: "I was wondering if you would share my resume with your network because I am looking for a new job in [specific field]." NO! Never email a recruiter this way. First, you are asking someone you don't know to champion you without them knowing if you are a good employee. Second, you are asking someone else to do your job search. You need to build the relationship. Your only thought should be how you can help a recruiter fill a specific role.

2. The recruiter has posted a job that matches your overall skill set. If you see a post that is perfect for your skill set, your resume is ready and your message is clear, and you have already applied online, you can alert the recruiter to your interest.

Say No to Gimmicks

When I was applying for my first job, I was told to use a gimmick like sending chocolate with my resume or attaching my resume to a pizza box. Back in 1992, the country was coming out of a recession, so jobs weren't easy to find. I did try, and not one of my "gimmicks" worked. And yet today, 30 years later, I've seen these same gimmicks and many others from people hoping to catch a recruiter's attention. Recruiters have reported gimmicks such as receiving a resume with shoes in a shoebox from a candidate trying to "get his foot in the door" to getting donuts with a note saying, "Donut miss this opportunity to interview me." Sure, recruiters and staff may chuckle at how "funny" the gesture was, but rarely will a candidate receive a call no matter how original the gimmick. They can look desperate and silly and make a recruiter feel uncomfortable. A gimmick will never advance your candidacy. Most recruiters enjoy the laugh but then move on. Therefore, save your money or spend it on a resume writer if you need help attracting recruiters' attention.

Even in the world of "viral" media, you will end up realizing that it wasn't the gimmick as much as the relationships that worked. You may have read about a Silicon Valley homeless man, David Cesarez, who put on a shirt and tie and stood on a busy road with a sign, "Homeless, hungry 4 success. Take a resume." A person took his picture and posted it on Twitter. It immediately went viral; he received more than 200 job offers, and he accepted a job at White Fox Defense.[2] The reason his stunt went viral wasn't only because he was standing on a road in a suit and tie but because his resume was clear, showing his experience and professionalism.[3] Further, when he interviewed for the job, he was prepared to discuss his experience and the value he could bring to a company. Based on his Twitter message about landing the job, it appears that numerous people rallied behind him to help him land at White Fox—people he had built relationships with. While he was "found" on the side of the road, in the end, his relationships were instrumental in him landing a job, not the gimmick.

Relationships with Recruiters

A final note about your relationship with recruiters. You are rarely the only applicant in play. In an effort to sell a candidate on a job and a company, recruiters are friendly, listen, and work hard to excite you about an opportunity. But since they aren't working for *you*, you are likely not the only person they are talking to no matter how perfect or enthusiastic you are for the role. Why? Because the company may not meet your salary requirements, your current employer may fight to keep you and you decide to stay, you may be a wrong culture fit, or you may simply be the second-best candidate for reasons you are not privy to. If you are a #2, stay in touch with the recruiter and/or the hiring manager because you may be a #1 in the future. That's what happened to me at Intuitive. I was rejected for the first role I applied to simply because someone else was a better fit for that client group, but days later the recruiter reached back out and had another opportunity to discuss. That opportunity became my next job. Recruiters may not technically work for you, but they are certainly your most important relationship when trying to land your next role.

Chapter 6 Summary

1. **Types of recruiters:** Know what type of recruiter you are talking to—internal, external, executive—and understand their role in the hiring process.

2. **Make yourself easy to find:** Create an open pathway to recruiters by opening up your LinkedIn Profile to new opportunities, responding to all inquiries even if you aren't interested, and applying to all jobs that interest you as soon as you see the opening.

3. **Make transferrable skills noticeable:** Use key words on LinkedIn and in your resume.

4. **Find connections:** Once you have applied online, look for direct or indirect connections to the posted position or company and reach out to the recruiter (if known) or anyone who can refer you to the role.

Resume Formatting

"Simple can be harder than complex: You have to work hard to get your thinking clean to make it simple. But it's worth it in the end because once you get there, you can move mountains."

—Steve Jobs, Apple co-founder

Fancy colors, divider lines, cool shapes, shading, and formatting with Employment, Education, and Skills in one column and the rest of your experience in the other. You spend hours making your resume look "pretty," and yet no one is calling you. That's because your resume either has no applicable substance to the job description, the message wasn't clear, you had typos or grammatical mistakes, or that pretty formatting messed it up in the Applicant Tracking System.

Keep It Simple

Recruiters and hiring managers don't care about fancy pictures or formatting. Even if you are in the creative field, like an art director, your experience will speak for itself in your portfolio. The overall format simply needs to be clean with enough white space for balance, easily scanned, and contain information that convinces a recruiter you have the experience and skills for the role. Remember: Recruiters review resumes for an average of seven seconds, so they aren't actually reading it; they are looking for key skills that match the job description.

Tip #7: Simple, clean resume format is the best format.

The first step is to get out of your head. Creating a resume that attracts attention causes anxiety because a lot rides on it and you can get caught up in how to format it. What goes first, education or experience? How many pages should it be? Should I add color and a design? How do I show that an employer has been acquired or that I held numerous roles at one company? Before digging into the best way to highlight transferable skills on your resume, let's get the basic formatting questions out of the way. You can find some answers online or in resume books, but it always amazes me how often the most professional and high-level executives can't format their resume in a way that reflects their strengths and skills in an easy-to-read format. So, don't skip this chapter!

Basic Formatting

1. How many pages? More pages will not equate to more experience or make your resume "better." I like to use "The rule of ten": If you have more than ten years' experience and multiple employers, you may have a two-page resume. If you have ten years experience and one or two employers over your entire career, then you should be able to fit your resume on one page. If you have less than ten years experience, your resume should be one page. No matter whether it is one or two pages, fill it up with substantive information but not a laundry list of every possible task or accomplishment. Resumes should only show the specific experiences and/or skills that are relevant to the job you're applying for.

2. White space. White space in a resume is critical. That means you need a proper header and footer (no less than .6 inch in Word) and white space on both sides of your resume (no less than .7 inch) for nice clean margins. The middle of your resume should have proper spacing of at least one space or 1.5 spaces between each subject section (e.g., between the end of the Experience section and the start of the Education section) and between each job, which can be slightly less. In short, the resume should be easy to glance at, not read.

3. Font. Calibri, Arial, and Candara are all fine. Arial tends to take up more space if you need to fill up your resume while Calibri is smaller.

Stay away from cursive (Lucinda) or fancy-looking (Harrington) fonts. No one cares what font you use as long as it's consistent throughout your resume and easy to read. Font size should never be less than 11 for the main content. For headers, consider 14 or 16 if you have room.

4. Grammar/punctuation. Using proper grammar and punctuation is obviously important. If you don't know how to use a semicolon, don't (and I find that most people *don't* know how to use it!). Given today's emphasis on email and texting, we write more than we talk, and so if you aren't a good writer or English is a second language, ask a friend or hire someone to rewrite and/or review your resume. You can also use Grammarly, which reviews and edits your writing, grammar, and punctuation and can spice up commonly used verbs and adjectives. It can also provide input on the tone of your cover letter. As for bullet points of success and roles under a job title, some people write sentence fragments, which don't require periods. I personally like periods at the end of each bullet point. The choice is yours; just be consistent.

5. Color. Should you highlight some words in color like your name or job titles? You can, but it's optional. Find one that is pleasing on the eyes and bold but not startling. Red is startling and also hard to read. Some blues are too bright. Color should be used sparingly and, again, consistently. If you highlight one job title, make sure all of them are the same color.

6. Capitals, bold, underlines. There are no rules about what and how to emphasize something, but too many emphases can clutter a resume. Be discerning and be consistent. If you bold the title of your job on one line, then do it with every job title. If you underline the company you work for, you should underline every previous company.

7. Chronological or skills based. Always default to a chronological resume because it will always work better in an ATS and it clearly shows your career history and path. That said, most ATSs allow you to both input the data chronologically and attach a skills-based resume if that's a better way to showcase your transferrable skills. Consider using a skills-based resume if you've had multiple terminations, you've changed jobs multiple times, but the core skills are the same (e.g., TV news reporting), there is no other way to highlight transferable skills, or you have long gaps in your resume.

Chronological resumes should show work experience in descending order with the most current job at the top and each prior job following in order by date. Some people have multiple freelance jobs. The one that is most current or most relevant to the job you're applying for should be first. Also, some people have a "volunteer job" that is more relevant than their "day job." Whether you are paid for a job or work full-time or part-time doesn't matter when it comes to job order. The most relevant job with the most current date that showcases applicable skills should always be first.

8. Home address. There is no reason to include your address on your resume. In Los Angeles, if you live in Silver Lake but apply for a job in Santa Monica, putting your address on your resume may exclude you when the recruiter thinks about commuting time. You don't want a recruiter to make that decision for you before you've had a chance to explain how you love long commutes or would be willing to move closer for the role. Further, if a job doesn't include relocation expense support, you may be dismissed even if you were willing to move on your own. What if your cell phone number is Los Angeles but you want to show you live in San Francisco where the position is located? How will a recruiter know you don't need a relocation package? Put the city/state next to each role; your most recent or current role should say San Francisco, CA.

9. Name, email, phone, and social media.
Name: If your name is Robert and you go by Bobby, put Bobby on your resume. When you apply online and fill in ATS information, enter Robert and, under Nickname, Bobby. If your nickname is "cute" like Sweetpea, use your real name. And make sure that your name is a bigger font size than the rest of the resume. It doesn't need to be 72, but at least 16.

Email: If you are like me and have an old AOL email address for junk mail, don't use it for your resume. Upgrade to a Gmail address or something more current because AOL, Yahoo!, and older addresses may show your age and unfortunately age discrimination still happens. Your email should also be professional. Don't use your high school "fun" address, such as bigdog@xxxx.com or sexyAlexa@xxxx.com, which doesn't show workplace maturity. Also, don't use your college email address even if you haven't graduated, because you want to show you have "moved on" to a professional email. Finally, consider creating an email address just for job searching so you won't miss any critical emails that come in. Recruiters often reach out via email first to see if you respond and to coordinate a time to speak.

Phone: This should be your cell phone. Don't worry if the prefix is from a different city/state where you currently live. Mobility is common these days and recruiters don't worry about the number they are calling to reach you.

Social media: Include a hyperlink to your LinkedIn profile, using the word "LinkedIn." The only time you would add Instagram, Facebook, or other platforms is when you are applying for a job that requires social media use (e.g., marketing) or savvy.

Putting It All Together

All contact information should be on the second line or grouped together. You don't have to write "email" and then write your email or "phone" before your phone number. However, you can separate them by a symbol like a circle, square, or diamond. Add a hyperlink to your LinkedIn profile. Here are two examples:

First & Last Name
myname@gmail.com • 310-555-5555 • LinkedIn

---

or

First & Last Name
myname@gmail.com ◆ 310-555-5555 ◆ LinkedIn

Contact information can also be grouped if it's clean and readable:

First & Last Name

myname@gmail.com
310-555-5555
LinkedIn

---

10. The line. It's nice to put a divider line under your contact information. Whether you do a single, double, thick, thin—it's your choice! And it's fine not to have one.

11. Full-perimeter page borders. Not necessary, but if you want one, go right ahead.

12. "Legally eligible" to work in the United States. When you apply online, the Applicant Tracking System will ask this question. That said, if you have a concern that you may not be considered for a role because your name is unique, your work experience is mostly outside the U.S., or your last job was outside the U.S., it doesn't hurt to add the words "Legally eligible to work in the United States" along with your contact information. Example:

First & Last Name
myname@gmail.com • 310-555-5555 • LinkedIn
Legally eligible to work in the United States

---

or

> **First & Last Name**
>
> myname@gmail.com
> 310-555-5555
> LinkedIn
> Legally eligible to work in the United States

13. Objective v. summary. Your resume should start with a strong statement of who you are. This is not an objective; your objective is to get a job. And don't title it with "Summary" or anything else that is redundant to the statement. It should relate directly to the job you are applying for using key words from the job description; it is not a generic statement about what you've accomplished. How to craft such an opening will be explored in the next chapter. A formatting example looks like this:

> **First & Last Name**
> myname@gmail.com • 310-555-5555 • LinkedIn
>
> **PRODUCT MARKETING THOUGHT LEADER** with a blend of technical, business, and marketing skills and a proven track record in engaging customers to drive business growth through designing and implementing innovative go-to-market strategies, sales initiatives, and campaigns across all verticals.

14. "Expertise," "highlights," "accomplishments," or "contributions." This is an optional addition to your list of specific positions. If you have 20 years' experience, or you need to fill white space on your resume because you've only had one or two jobs, or you want to show soft skills that you haven't been able to work into the rest of your resume, or you want to catch a recruiter's eye with key words from the job description, consider summarizing your overall accomplishments in bullet points after the summary paragraph. You can call this section any of the suggested headers at the beginning of this paragraph depending on what you choose to emphasize. For example:

Expertise

- Product marketing
- GTM strategies
- Managing teams
- Competitive research
- B2B targeting
- Performance optimization
- Customer acquisition
- Customer journey development
- Digital analytics

This section can also focus more on soft skills or a combination of hard and soft skills for someone who doesn't have a lot of work experience.

Highlights

- Self-starter
- GTM strategist
- Team player
- PR campaign driver
- Cognitively flexible leader
- EQ communicator
- Creative storyteller
- Collateral developer
- Data researcher

Yet another way to approach this section is to highlight three to five key accomplishments or contributions over the course of your entire career. Note that this covers both hard and soft skills:

Key Contributions

➢ **Product Marketing**—Drove go-to-market strategies including positioning, implementation, and messaging for B2B and B2C products across all verticals and determined data touchpoints for analysis on performance.

➢ **Performance Optimization**—Generated more than 50% uplift in revenue from defining measurement objectives and strategy, analyzing large and small data sets, and translating complex insights to inform key decisions regarding performance in support of business goals.

> **Leading Cross-functional Teams**—Empowered U.S. bi-coastal and international teams through emotionally intelligent coaching and provided overall continuous improvement with employee growth and engagement resulting in no team attrition over a ten-year period.

All of these examples show the expertise, core skills, highlights or contributions in a section near the top of a resume but can also be captured in a left column on a resume. Specifically applicants who want one resume to capture expertise for tangential roles may want to list all "Expertise" or "Core Skills" in a separate column down the left side of a resume so the resume can be tailored slightly per application.

15. Experience. Which comes first, the job title or company name where you work (or worked)? Lead with the company name if

→ the company you work for is prominent like Google or IBM.

→ the company you are applying to is a direct competitor or comparable to the company you are working at.

→ you are transitioning careers and your current title is completely different from the role you are pursuing or there is no way to adjust your current title to make it directly relevant (see more below).

→ you are early in your career and only have entry-level titles (e.g., "specialist" or "coordinator").

→ you've had multiple titles at any one company (from promotions or changing roles).

Example of how it should look:

IBM, Armonk, NY
Marketing Specialist

Start with your title if none of the above are true and

→ the companies you have worked for are not well known to the average person.

- ➔ the job title you currently have matches the job title of the position open.

- ➔ your company was acquired and your job title stayed the same.

- ➔ you have years of experience and are considered senior in your field.

Examples would be:

Vice President, Content Marketing
IBM, Armonk, NY

or

Marketing Specialist
Bobbledeboo, Inc., Jennison, TN

If you meet multiple criteria regarding both title and company name (e.g., you have a big title and you work for a well-known company), I suggest starting with the title first to show you are at the level of the new position or it's the logical next step in your career. The one exception is if you have held numerous jobs at the same company and/or have been promoted in your current role; then it would be easier to lead with the name of the company. I'll demonstrate why below.

Title: If your title doesn't match the job you are applying for, you can change it slightly to make it relevant. My title at Viacom was VP, Business & Legal Affairs, Labor & Employment, Production Risk Team. It was too long to put on a resume and would not have been directly relevant to the HR Business Partner roles I was applying for. Most recruiters would have dismissed me as "just a lawyer." But I was a business partner every day to leaders at all levels in the company, so I shortened it to "Production Risk Business Partner," which captured the essence of the work. When asked if I worked in HR, my answer was clear: "No. I report up through the legal department, but I work as a business partner to leaders throughout the organization cross-functionally, including . . ." Be careful not to cross the line into a lie.

Multiple titles, same company: If you have been promoted, fantastic! That shows you have grown at your company. In that case, the company will always be first so you can list your numerous jobs under it:

Bobbledeboo, Inc., Jennison, TN	6/14–Current
VP, Content Marketing Strategy & Analytics (promoted)	8/17–Current
Sr. Director, Content Marketing (promoted)	4/16–7/17
Director, Content Marketing	6/14–3/16

Company was acquired multiple times: If you stayed with a company that changed names multiple times, then list your title first, each company, and then years of employment, distinguishing which companies were acquired:

VP, Content Marketing Strategy & Analytics	6/14–Current
Bobbledeboo, Inc., Jennison, TN	
Bobble Co, Inc. (acquired)	4/16–7/17
Deboo, Inc. (acquired)	6/14–3/16

Unemployment through bankruptcy: If you are unemployed because something like a bankruptcy happened to the company, spell it out to the recruiter why you are unemployed:

Data Analyst	6/15–9/19
Bobbledeboo, Inc. (defunct through bankruptcy)	

or

Data Analyst	6/15–9/19
Bobbledeboo, Inc. (defunct)	

Unemployment through reduction in force (RIF): Many companies do mass layoffs as they reorganize for efficiency each year. If you were a casualty of this, own it.

Data Analyst	6/15–9/19
Bobbledeboo, Inc.	

- ▸ Provide insights into performance of marketing campaigns to drive results toward business goals including projects on [X, Y, Z].
- ▸ Reduction in force during consolidation of departments eliminated this role.

Temp work for a company through a third-party agency: If you work as a temporary worker or as a freelance worker, you may go to one company every day for work but you are truly employed through a third party. Use the actual employer (the agency) in the ATS but list the company(ies) that benefited from your work on your resume:

Social Media Manager (full-time freelance)   6/18–Current
Bobbledeboo, Inc. through ABC Agency

or

Social Media Manager   6/18–Current
Bobbledeboo, Inc. through ABC Agency (full-time contractor)

Dates of employment: There is no right way to format dates, but they should go on the right-hand side as shown above and should not be bold or underlined. Dates provide two pieces of data: How many years' experience you have in a specific area and/or whether you change jobs often. Your career history should dictate how you format your dates.

Standard dates include month/year such as 6/2017–6/2020 or 6/17–6/20 for someone who is employed. You can also use spelled-out months if you like that look better: September 2019–June 2020. If you have a long title, you may need to use the shortest date format. Either way, be consistent with use of hyphens or dashes between dates.

For longer unemployment gaps, consider just putting years on your resume instead of month/year such as 2017–2018. You may have finished your last job in May 2018, but having 2018 instead of the month will appear at first glance that you worked to the end of the year and a recruiter won't be as inhibited from calling and inquiring further. Whichever format you choose, be consistent throughout your resume.

Experience timeline: Some people recommend listing no more than 15 years' experience on a resume. That makes sense if you have relevant experience over the past 15 years. It also makes sense if you are concerned about age discrimination. There is no hard rule on this. My experience goes back more than 25 years including my first career as a TV news reporter, which lasted for more than a decade. It's a great conversation piece and I have never interviewed without someone asking me about it. Further, I can apply it to any role since I gained presentation and communication skills that relate to executive presence while working under tight deadlines in fast-paced environments. You need to be first in TV news! If your jobs show skills that are relevant beyond 15 years, it is fine to leave them on your resume. However, consider combining multiple roles if you did the same or similar jobs for multiple companies. Here is how I present my TV news experience:

KFOR, KWTV, WTIC, WDTN, WNDU, KDRV   4/92–3/02
Consumer Investigative/General Assignment Reporter, Nationwide

▶ Developed, researched, investigated, wrote, and reported on air award-winning general assignment, consumer, investigative, and legal stories for ABC, NBC, and CBS affiliates in Oklahoma City, Oklahoma; South Bend, Indiana; Hartford, Connecticut; Dayton, Ohio; and Medford, Oregon.

Even in the above example, my employers are still in descending order with the most recent TV station I worked at first. This type of combining can also be used with as few as two employers if the title is the same or similar and the summary of the work performed is clear. In the example below, I worked as a legal clerk or intern in both jobs:

New Line Cinema / McKinney Stringer, P. C.   8/01–8/02
Legal Clerk, Los Angeles, CA, and Oklahoma City, OK

▶ Researched topics including but not limited to employment issues and other entertainment and business-related issues for New Line Cinema executives (6/02–8/02) and employment cases including ERISA and HIPAA issues for managing partners at McKinney Stringer, P. C. (8/01–6/02).

Bullet points vs. paragraphs. All resumes should have bullet points under the job title/company. Some resumes also feature a sentence under each job title describing the business or the overall nature of the job.

Bobbledeboo, Inc., Jennison, TN   6/14–Current
Fast-growing startup that connects mission-based advertisers with
platform opportunities.

A descriptor sentence is fine if the company isn't well known and
you want to relate it to the company you are applying to (e.g., you are
relating your current work to a job at a digital advertising company). You
may also use that brief statement as a quick summary of your applicable
skills. That said, I don't recommend it and believe the "type of company"
you work for can fit within the first bullet point. Extra lines mean extra
reading. Your experience is more critical than what your company sold
for or whether it's in the Fortune 500. For example:

Bobbledeboo, Inc., Jennison, TN   6/14–Current
Vice President, Sales Strategy & Operations (promoted)
Sr. Director, Sales Strategy & Operations

▸ Led both a team of three in designing scalable processes to support
  4x growth of sales as well as sales support teams tasked in part
  with influencing the executive team in annual planning, resource
  allocation, and key components of sales-commission plans at this
  party favor start-up.

How many bullet points should each job have? At least two for jobs
of more than 10 years old and at least three for jobs that are less than 10
years old. Further, each bullet point should start with an active verb (i.e.,
"Led," "Drove," "Spearheaded," "Managed," or "Facilitated") instead of a
passive one ("Responsible for").

Location: You may have noticed that the location of each job has fluctuated in the above examples between the top and second line. Sometimes
it is next to the company and sometimes it's next to the job title. There is
no hard rule; it should go where it fits best. Location only communicates
whether you are an in-state candidate or may require a relocation package. For foreign nationals, it proves you are currently working in the U.S.
and legally eligible to work in the U.S.

16. Education. Education today means a lot less than it did just a few years ago. In late 2018, Glassdoor compiled a list of companies no longer requiring a college degree for certain high-level jobs, which included Apple, Penguin Random House, Google, Bank of America, Home Depot, and IBM. College is a great time to grow up, learn what you want to do, and gain some work experience, but companies are starting to realize that the right experience is as important as education if not more so. Going to an Ivy League school shows you either have the capacity to learn and the drive to succeed or your family has deep pockets. (Not trying to insult!) That said, I firmly believe that education should come after experience. Experience gets you the job; education is more of a "connection" or a "talking point." Some people disagree with me on this and your resume will not be rejected because you put education first. Here are some examples where that makes sense:

→ You are a recent graduate who went to a top-ten school such as Harvard, Yale, or Stanford. You have an exceptionally high GPA *and* you don't have a lot of relevant work experience. For example, you went on work-study to put yourself through school, so your resume is full of security or library intake jobs. Kudos to you. Work-study takes grit!

→ You went to a top school in your location such as UC Berkeley near San Francisco or UCLA or USC in Los Angeles and you are seeking work in the same city *but* you don't have a lot of relevant work experience.

→ You know someone at the company where you are applying who is an alumnus from your school *and* you have a high GPA (3.5 or above).

Education should always be listed with the school first followed by the degree underneath in descending chronological order:

University of California, Los Angeles   5/2019
Master of Business Administration, GPA 3.6

University of California, Los Angeles   5/2015
BA Communication, GPA 4.0

Again—and it's worth repeating: I firmly believe that education goes after experience on a resume even if you don't have much of a work history. Why? Because this book is teaching you how to make whatever experiences you do have relevant to the field you want to move into.

GPA. There is no reason to list your GPA unless it is above a 3.5 and you graduated in the past three years. Otherwise leave it off. Most companies don't care about GPA and if it is important, the recruiter will ask you for it.

Activities/Clubs. New graduates should only list activities if they are relevant to the type of jobs you are applying for and you need to fill your resume. All diversity clubs are relevant. Nonintramural college sports are relevant because they show that a candidate has competitive spirit and understands discipline and the value of hard work. Clubs associated with communication are relevant. If your resume is already filled with internships, just list the name of the school and the degree, and try to add key words and relevant skills based on your involvement in clubs. For example:

University of California, Los Angeles   May 2015
BA Communication

- ▸ **Treasurer, Communications Club**—Managed P&L, all membership dues, accounts payable and receivable, and kept the club within the annual budget.

- ▸ **Volunteer, Big Buddy Mentor Program**—Gained an appreciation for diversity and differences while mentoring special needs men and women in basic life skills such as balancing a checkbook, paying a tip, and social interactions.

- ▸ **Member, Omega Psi Phi Fraternity, Inc. (Black Law Student Association)**—Participated in events that educated employers about the advancement of diversity in the workplace.

17. Skills proficiencies. If you are creating a skills-based resume or if you are a new graduate or you don't have an Expertise/Highlights section or you haven't performed certain skills within your roles but you have expertise or proficiency in them, list them either under education or at the end of the resume under "Additional Skills" or "Skills Proficiencies" or just "Skills" if they are directly relevant and listed in the job description. For example:

Skills Proficiencies

▶ MS Office including Excel, Outlook, PowerPoint, One Note, Cloud Computing

Or if you are applying for a data science role:

Technical Proficiencies

▶ SQL, Python, Java, Scala, R, Julia, C++

18. Awards/Published articles/Blogs. Include these under the job or school where you received or published them. If you are transitioning between jobs, list only those published articles or awards that are directly applicable to the job you are applying for. Publishing articles on LinkedIn doesn't count unless that's a requirement of the prospective job. Blogging doesn't count unless it will be part of the prospective job or the blog posts are relevant to the prospective job. These should not be listed in a separate section; better to fit them under the employer or school (just like your activities above) depending on when you published, unless you need to fill up space on your resume.

19. Hobbies/Interests/Volunteer work. These do not belong on a resume. In general, recruiters and hiring managers don't care whether you love to cook, like to travel, or are building your own tiny home. Outside hobbies mean you aren't focused on work. Keep them to yourself unless they come up during the interview process. Volunteer work can be used as a job under "Experience" if you are transitioning from, say, being a stay-at-home parent or being unemployed or that experience is more relevant with transferrable skills to the job you are applying to than the job you currently have. (More on this in Chapter 10.)

What to *Not* Put on Your Resume

→ **Pictures.** Never put a picture of yourself on your resume. It can lead to unintentional bias by the recruiter or hiring manager. Also, it's just creepy. You're not dating; you're looking for a job! That's what LinkedIn is for and, yes, you should have a picture on LinkedIn.

→ **Tables, charts, diagrams, graphs, graphics, tables, text boxes, icons.** The ATS will not interpret these correctly and could garble the rest of the information.

→ **First- or third-person sentences.** Never use "I," "she," "he," "me," or "my." Everyone knows it is your resume, so this is unnecessary. The only time you would use these is if you would like to put the gender pronoun you identify with next to your name.

→ **Proprietary/confidential information.** This could be anything such as sales-rate cards or company revenue. Use percentages instead (e.g., achieved 110% of goal).

→ **References.** Don't add reference contact information to a resume or "References Available Upon Request." Of course they are! Just have your references ready for when they ask you for them (more on this in Chapter 15).

→ **High school.** Don't list your high school unless you didn't go to college. If you don't have a bachelor's degree and the job requires it, leave education completely off your resume. If you started college but didn't finish, put the college on your resume and dates attended, but do not put the degree on your resume or it will be deceiving to the recruiter unless you add anticipated date of graduation unless you add anticipated date of graduation.

Your resume or LinkedIn profile will be the very first interaction a recruiter has with you. Your resume should be neat, in the proper order, consistently formatted, and free of grammatical and spelling errors. Ask friends to look at it from a "format only" perspective to make sure it is easy to glance at for seven seconds. Then test a family member on what they learned in that short period of time to make sure your message is clear. Once clear and full of substantive, relevant information, your resume will be ready to submit to a prospective job.

Chapter 7 Summary

1. **Keep it simple:** Don't add fancy fonts or a lot of color. The best resumes are simple and clean with a lot of white space.

2. **One or two pages:** No resume, no matter how many years of experience you have, should exceed two pages. Don't put every accomplishment on your resume—just the most relevant ones.

3. **Experience in descending order:** All jobs should be listed with the most current position first and the oldest last.

4. **Feature both hard and soft skills:** Add a summary and/or a section with expertise, highlights, or key contributions to make sure all key words for the role have been included.

Setting Your Resume's Substantive Theme

"When I let go of what I am, I become what I might be."

—Lao Tzu, Chinese philosopher

Most people draft resumes based on their past experience and define themselves by their professional accomplishments. But you are reading this book because you don't want to look backward; you want to look forward and move into a new career. Therefore, you should create your resume using the lens of the job you are applying for in the career you want to pursue. Since you have never worked in that new career, the job description will be your guide.

Dissect the Job Description

Job descriptions hold the key to what is most important in your targeted position. Two companies may post the same title for a position, but the roles and responsibilities may be vastly different. For example, two people say, "I want a delicious fruit dessert." One asks for a slice of apple pie and the other wants a bowl of berries. Or one wants apple pie with a big scoop of vanilla ice cream and the other wants apple pie with extra cinnamon and nutmeg. When you read job descriptions, you need to identify the most important skills needed for the role and then design your resume according to the company's expectations and needs. A generic resume with everything you've ever done ignores the specific needs of the new job. It either won't be read or could be viewed negatively by a recruiter who questions your focus or whether you

Tip #8: Use the opening sentence to grab attention.

have relevant skills. Once you find the positions you want, your mission is to determine who you are in relation to those job descriptions and present an alignment.

A "summary of skills" on your resume explains who you are professionally, what you can do, and how successful you are at doing it. It is about positioning your achievements through the lens of the new role so others can see how your unique skills are applicable. Also helpful is an "introductory statement." While some recruiters may skip over this sentence, none have ever rejected a resume because it is there, and when transitioning careers, it can be a strategic opening. This sentence should grab the recruiters' attention and motivate them to read the rest of the resume. How do you craft a strong, authentic, opening statement defining who you are and what you can/want to do? Here are three easy steps:

1. Dissect the job description for hard and soft skills. Print out each job description and highlight all the relevant skills it emphasizes. Hard skills include actual experience such as SQL expertise or building marketing campaigns or specialized knowledge in a specific industry such as biotech or gaming. Soft skills represent the "how" of a job such as "self-starter" and "able to work cross-functionally."

When reading the sample job description below, notice the **bold for hard skills**, <u>underline for soft skills</u>, and *italics* for words to potentially use in the cover letter:

<u>Sr. Manager, Product Marketing</u>
Company is looking for a hardcore **product marketing** <u>leader</u> to **design and implement go-to-market strategies** for our *industry-leading technology solutions*. You will establish Company's position as a <u>thought leader</u> in the **SaaS industry** by **creating compelling market positioning** and be responsible for **creating persuasive sales initiatives and campaigns ranging from cloud-connected**

messaging to vertical market solutions. You will also **develop collateral from concept to publishing.**

You must be a <u>highly motivated</u> and <u>dedicated</u> marketer and <u>self-starter</u> who is comfortable in a *dynamic, fast-paced environment* and who possesses <u>strong execution skills</u> and <u>enjoys being part of a team</u>. You must have the unique ability to **identify new opportunities to grow the business.** You will be **building, leading, and motivating a team.** You are expected to be a <u>stellar communicator</u> capable of **engaging customers and partners and evangelizing our product.** This is a *high-visibility position* that requires a **blend of strong technical, business, and marketing skills.**

Once you've dissected the job description, you will have the information you need to highlight in your summary statement.

Title Yourself

2. How do you want to "label" yourself? Are you a leader? A specialist? Your current "title"? There are many ways to start this first sentence, but if you look at the job description, the soft skills will give you the answer. In fact, you have choices: "thought leader," "dedicated marketer," "self-starter and highly motivated," "strong execution skills" ("doer"), "enjoys being part of a team" ("team player"), "stellar communicator." "Thought leader" would be hard to use for someone who is new to the workforce or that industry, but could be used by someone with at least five years' experience doing strategic work in any field. "Dedicated," "Self-starter," "Highly motivated," "Team player," and "Stellar communicator" could be used by anyone who believes those are applicable characteristics. The object is to find the strongest, legitimate version of you and lead your resume with those critical first words. Examples:

→ For someone who wants to stay in product marketing but move to a new role:

Product Marketing Thought Leader . . .

→ For someone in product management (e.g., engineering) who has a creative bent or a role that interacts with product marketers and wants to move to product marketing:

Product Thought Leader or Innovative, Cross-Functional Leader

→ For someone with no experience or who has some internship experience:

"Highly motivated, detail-oriented self-starter . . . "

Note that "detail oriented" is not in the job description. That's fine! It's a great skill to have in any job.

3. Incorporate hard and soft skills into your summary statement. Incorporate all relevant hard skills from the job description into your summary. If you aren't experienced or transitioning to a new career, focus on your soft skills but add a few hard skills. Examples (bold and underlined only to show correlating hard and soft skills respectively):

→ For the experienced marketer who wants to move to a new type of marketing job:

Marketing thought leader with a **blend of technical, business, and product marketing skills** who has a proven track record in **engaging customers** and **driving business growth** through **designing and implementing innovative go-to-market strategies** and **creating persuasive sales initiatives and campaigns** across all **verticals.**

→ For the product management (engineering) executive who wants to move into product marketing:

Product thought leader in the **SaaS industry** with a **blend of technical, business, and marketing skills** who has a proven track record of <u>influencing cross-functional teams</u>, guiding **marketing strategies** and contributing to **persuasive sales initiatives and campaigns** that drive **business growth.**

→ For the person who works in finance (or any other field) in a SaaS-focused company and wants to move into marketing:

Highly Visible SaaS Leader with a **blend of technical and business savvy in cloud-connected messaging and vertical market solutions** who has a proven track record of **identifying and developing new opportunities to drive business growth.**

Grab Attention

The first sentence should grab a recruiter's attention. There is no perfect format, but the intent should be to make "who you are" and the skills you will bring stand out. Therefore, while there is no rule, consider highlighting the first few words such as in "SMALL CAPS" or "ALL CAPS" font and/ or making the font slightly bigger for those first few words. Such style changes will give your first sentence some pop and make it stick out. In the example below, the first few words are in SMALL CAPS at 13 pt. font size followed by plain 12 pt. font size.

First & Last Name
myname@gmail.com • 310-555-5555 • LinkedIn

PRODUCT MARKETING THOUGHT LEADER with a blend of technical, business, and marketing skills and a proven track record in engaging customers to drive business growth through designing and implementing innovative go-to-market strategies, sales initiatives, and campaigns across all verticals.

After you write this sentence, own it. That is who you are, how you will characterize yourself in interviews, and how you will establish yourself when you transition careers. If you can't yet own it, reflect back on your true values. What is missing? What will truly represent who you are and your values? What will reflect your true skills? Tweak it until you feel comfortable that your skills, values, and capabilities are accurately and compellingly presented.

Choose Applicable Skills

When I was an entertainment lawyer in the production risk department at Viacom and I wanted to transition to a Human Resources Business Partner position, I spent weeks looking at similar roles online. I noticed that some of them were more tactically oriented while others seemed more strategic. Some mentioned "coaching" while others emphasized employee relations. Some were full-service HR Business Partner roles covering organizational design, talent management, career development, workforce planning, and performance reviews while others were narrower with just a few of those areas. I also looked up my HR Business Partner friends on LinkedIn to see what they wrote on their pages. As I narrowed down the areas I had experience in and the ones I would need experience in, I knew I had to use some key words to attract a recruiter and hiring a manager. This is where I landed (key words in bold):

> **STRATEGIC LEADER** with a track record of **solving complex organizational challenges** through **people-related solutions** that enhance **organizational effectiveness** and efficiencies, manage competing interests, and **build relationships** while bridging differences, resulting in **increased performance** and sustained **cross-organizational impact.**

Notice that my summary statement didn't mention "HR Business Partner" because I wasn't one. But I used key words that to me were all true. I used some of those capabilities cross-functionally and some just within our team and I created those outcomes. In looking at my experience through the lens of an HR role, I was able to show how my skills were directly applicable to the core concepts of HR.

Once you write that first sentence, the rest of your resume will flow. That sentence is your brand. It is who you are *today*. The rest of your resume should reflect the career you have chosen, not the jobs you left.

Chapter 8 Summary

1. **Set a theme:** Create a dynamic statement with the first sentence that explains who you are and what skills you have that make you a solid candidate for the role.

2. **Dissect job descriptions:** Look for hard and soft skills to use in the summary statement.

3. **Title yourself:** Determine the first few words that will label yourself in the strongest way and set the perception of how you will succeed in the job.

4. **Choose applicable skills:** Look at your current skills and responsibilities through the lens of the new role and pick out the most applicable to round out your first statement.

Highlighting Transferable Skills

"People with highly transferable skills may be specialists in certain areas, but they're also incredible generalists—something businesses that want to grow need."

—Leah Busque, TaskRabbit founder

The "Experience" section on your resume and LinkedIn profile is what attracts recruiters. Most resumes include a laundry list of everything a person has ever done, but that's not how to create an Experience section that stands out and attracts recruiters' interest beyond seven seconds. Experience is the most strategic section of a resume and should be used to showcase only those skills that are directly applicable to the prospective job. You may think that since you worked on an incredible project with a phenomenal outcome, it must be on your resume. But if that project isn't directly applicable to the job you are applying for and you can't find a way to make a case for it, it shouldn't be on your resume. Yes, I am asking you to leave off some of your greatest accomplishments because they will only muddle your resume and confuse a recruiter if they aren't directly relevant to the roles you are pursuing. I am also giving you permission to leave off your day-to-day job duties if they aren't directly applicable to the prospective job. This is hard advice for most people to follow because it begs the question: What DO I put on my resume?

Aligning Experience with Skills

In the same way you made your summary relate to the position you seek, determine how to make your "experience" relate to it. Print out the job description and look at the applicable skills, then make your experience align with those skills even if you don't have specific

Tip #9: Your resume should only contain information that is directly applicable to your new career.

experience with that particular job. Let's look at a transactional healthcare lawyer who spends the majority of her day negotiating contracts for hospitals and clinics but wants to move into policy/government affairs. Here are three considerations to make that transition easier:

1. Stay in the same or an analogous industry. Consider staying in the same industry because experience in areas such as healthcare, entertainment, or tech means you understand a certain industry that will help make your skills appear more easily transferable. For the healthcare lawyer who wants to move into a policy/government affairs role, she already knows the "lingo" of the healthcare industry and understands its inner workings. That will help make the transition to a new role easier than trying to change both industries *and* careers because the growth path seems more palatable to hiring managers. They only have to teach you the function, not "how the industry works."

If the same industry isn't possible, look for an analogous field. When I wanted to transition from lawyer to HR business partner, I had already moved to the San Francisco Bay Area. There were no traditional studios or entertainment companies near me. Every person I talked to said I should target Roku, GoPro, and EA. They weren't entertainment companies in the traditional Hollywood sense but were technology companies that centered around entertainment; Roku is about streaming entertainment, GoPro is about creating entertainment, EA is about gaming entertainment.

2. Review "experience needed." The best place to research this is through job descriptions and on the LinkedIn profiles of those who are already working in your chosen career. Looking online, the healthcare lawyer finds numerous job descriptions that interest her and, from them, compiles critical job requirements, highlighting the most important skills (**bold** for hard skills, <u>underline</u> for soft skills, and *italics* for information to use in a cover letter):

> ▶ Manage ongoing efforts and **communications to educate members of Congress, congressional staff, and relevant agencies and their staff** about patient, clinical, and <u>*economic value as well as impacts to society*</u>.
>
> ▶ Closely **monitor and flag legislative and regulatory actions** that would <u>*impact the company's operations and/or business goals*</u> in such realms as (but not limited to) **healthcare, taxation, trade, and reimbursement, and make appropriate recommendations to company leaders for action.**
>
> ▶ <u>Promote company's point of view about policies</u> in these areas to policymakers.
>
> ▶ <u>Provide strategic direction and oversight</u> to internal and external resources to ensure effective advocacy to promote, protect, and expand the business nationally.
>
> ▶ **Draft position papers, policy briefings, testimony, and comments on proposed legislative and regulatory actions.**
>
> ▶ **Collaborate and coordinate with relevant trade associations.**
>
> ▶ **JD** or **PAC** experience a plus, but not required.

3. Match your skills. Match your experience to the job description requirements as closely as possible using the STAR method: Situation, Task, Action, Result. *Situation* is the work being done or the challenge or issue that needs to be solved. *Task* describes the goal or what you want to achieve. *Action* is the work you did to bring about the solution and reach the goal. *Results* are the outcomes and measurement of those outcomes. The object is to incorporate as many pieces of STAR as you can into each bullet point of experience.

The healthcare lawyer needs to look at her old job and skill set through the lens of the new job. What key words from her targeted job descriptions and LinkedIn profiles relate to her current job duties? See how she showcases some of what she does through the lens of the new job by using those key words directly from the job description (**bold** for hard skills, <u>underline</u> for soft skills):

- Counsel nonprofit, for-profit, and governmental hospitals, healthcare systems, and physician groups on all aspects of **healthcare investments, operations, and regulatory matters,** achieving the <u>best patient, clinical, and economic value as well as impact to society</u>. (STAR)
- Closely **monitor and flag legislative and regulatory actions** that impact companies' operations and/or business goals in **healthcare, trade, reimbursement,** fraud/abuse, anti-trust, HIPAA, and privacy and **communicate appropriate recommendations to company leaders for action.**
- **Draft white papers on various areas of healthcare,** including [types of whitepapers], which provide clients continual access to information.
- **Advise and provide strategies to clients on lobbying efforts,** ensuring legislation continues to drive and accelerate the healthcare business. (STAR)

While the transactional attorney's main role in her current job is to draft contracts, nowhere in the above bullet points does it say, "Negotiate and draft contracts for hospitals, healthcare systems, physician groups, etc." Why? It's not relevant to the career she wants to move into. The above "experience" shows that this lawyer is in tune with healthcare regulations and legislation, understands how government works, and stays on top of matters that could affect business, even if it only represents 5% of her current position.

Again, her experiences don't lie. While the above states that she has worked with lobbyists, it doesn't say that she has direct contact with members of Congress or congressional staff or relevant agencies and their staff. But she does monitor regulations and legislation regularly to do her job well, which is how she will make that connection during the interview process. Finally, note that every bullet point doesn't conform to the STAR method and they don't need to. If you *can* point to results, add them as often as possible.

If this lawyer didn't have any regulatory or legislative experience to draw from, she may choose to take the next six months or so to gain that experience. That may include taking some meet/greets with government agency staff and/or becoming more knowledgeable about how agencies create regulations or lobby for legislation. She will make that determination from reviewing the necessary skills in the job description.

Here's another example: A software engineer who works in healthcare wants to move into human resources. That seems like a crazy big jump, right? Well, it all depends on the engineer's experience. His "engineering" resume experience may read like this:

> ▸ Implement business product innovations resulting in $1B+ revenue impact.
>
> ▸ Transform product portfolio to cloud based, enabling new business models through data analytics, machine learning/AI, and IoT.
>
> ▸ Build and deliver high-quality products within the constraints of financial, user experience, and security needs.
>
> ▸ Lead a global engineering team of 1,000 employees and contractors in five locations.
>
> ▸ Designed and launched new Singapore development center to establish offshore talent presence with local leadership.

But HR business partner roles require experience in **executive coaching, organizational design, workforce analytics (hiring/retention/ attrition), performance management, change management, employee engagement, diversity and inclusion, and organizational effectiveness.** Some roles prefer the PHR or SPHR, while other companies want to see the GPHR certification because they have or are expanding into a global workforce. Looking at his engineering work through an HR lens, he can focus on other accomplishments that he didn't have on his engineering resume but are directly applicable to HR:

► **Provide people leadership** to multiple R&D and engineering teams (≈1,000 engineers) in **diverse global locations (APAC, EMEA, LATAM)** including **coaching managers and employees** to amplify their contributions, resulting in **increased engagement** to learn new technologies (big data, mobile IoT) with an **attrition rate of <5% on all global teams.**

► **Develop and use data analytics** to drive operations and successfully **manage performance,** moving employees where **skills and strengths could be maximized in furtherance of business goals with 100% retention rate.**

► **Expand global team** including growing a Singapore Office from 10 to 200 employees, creating strategies for **employee competencies and experience levels,** and helping the office adopt **company culture and understand its role in the global corporation.**

► Drive **diversity and inclusion** by participating on company's diversity and inclusion council and spearheading "second innings" to identify opportunities for women who would like to return to the workforce after 4–6 years of family time, resulting in 32 women in four countries being hired.

► Guide supervisors through **change management** by encouraging deep understanding of change within the ecosystem, **creating the communication strategy, and influencing transparency in open forums cross-functionally** (sales, R&D, marketing), resulting in transformation of product portfolio from on-premise to cloud-based applications, which enabled new business models in data analytics, AI, and IoT.

► **Engage employees** by creating best-in-company events (annual family day, town halls) and developing employees' talents, resulting in a "top ten award" in engagement survey scores in a global organization.

The previous example shows that, as an engineer, he understands HR concepts from a managerial perspective. He also took the SPHR to show his dedication to moving into HR. A hiring manager with a growth mindset would see this knowledge and experience as a huge asset to any tech company seeking a technical HR Business Partner. Note: Nowhere does it say he works in HR, but refocusing his resume through the lens of HR shows he is performing specific HR-type functions while leading an engineering organization. Even though he had tremendous successes in launching revolutionary products while coming in millions under budget, such accomplishments are not directly relevant to HR. For those achievements, clink glasses of champagne with a friend while leaving them off your resume or they will become noise that distracts a recruiter from seeing your true value in the prospective job.

Chapter 9 Summary

1. **Same industry:** Consider staying in the same industry because your experience in specific areas such as healthcare, entertainment, or technology will help make those skills appear more transferable to a new career. And if not the same industry, look for an analogous field.

2. **Review job descriptions:** Determine what experience is needed to be successful in the new career/job.

3. **Match experience:** Only include experience on your resume that matches as closely as possible the requirements and key words in the job description, preferably using the STAR method.

Mind the Gap

"Life is a matter of choices, and every choice you make, makes you."

—John C. Maxwell, leadership author

Taking time off to raise a child or care for a sick family member. Taking time off to travel the world. Taking time off to figure out what you want to do after being fired or quitting a job. Taking time off to simply . . . breathe. It doesn't matter why someone takes time off from the commercial workforce. The choice was made and now it is time to own it and explain the gap on your resume. This gap brings a tremendous amount of anxiety and fear to those looking for that next opportunity. From coaching numerous stay-at-home parents and people who have been terminated from employment, I see how often the fear and lack of confidence show up.

The most important thing to do on a resume regarding a gap is to own it: You made a choice (or the choice was made for you) to take time off from the commercial workforce. Then determine how to best position it on your resume or whether it needs to be

Tip #10: Own the Gap

positioned at all. If you choose to leave a time gap unfilled in your resume, the recruiter and hiring manager will automatically speculate as to what the gap could be. The only way to prevent a recruiter from creating a false narrative or interpretation is to explain what happened clearly and succinctly on your resume since cover letters are rarely read.

Your resume is about marketing yourself in the best positive light, so the object is to find a way to show how that time off enhanced your qualifications for the job. By including the gap in your resume in a positive way, you will leave no room for inaccurate speculation. Think of it as a branding challenge: position that time off just as you would every other job you've had to make it relevant to the role you are applying to. Here are some common reasons why people take time off and examples of how to position it on your resume.

Stay-at-home Parent

As a mom, I know there is no harder job, but not all employers will see it that way. Therefore, determine what you did while you weren't working in the commercial workforce (because we all know you were certainly working!). Don't use cute titles such as "Domestic Engineer" or "Conflict Resolution Specialist" or "Chief Organizer" to describe your parental time. They will distract a recruiter from thinking you are serious about re-entering the workforce.

Consider whether any volunteer activities at your children's school are relevant to the roles you are interested in such as helping a teacher or being a treasurer for the school Harvest Fest or School Club. Volunteering is a legitimate way to keep skills fresh. On the resume, you can put the title and "employer" underneath to match the rest of the format along with bullet points showing what you actually did as it relates to the job you are applying for. (For those who volunteer without a specific role, the title would be "Volunteer.") The person below, for example, is applying for a finance job using a relevant volunteer role:

Volunteer Treasurer (or **Volunteer**)
Name of School, City
- ▸ Effectively managed $100,000 in monies raised through fundraising efforts including processing accounts receivable

---

and payable in a timely and accurate manner, ensuring that all payments are posted accurately.

► Investigated account discrepancies, settled bank accounts, posted and balanced financial data in a variety of ledgers with 100% accuracy.

► Set up various mobile payment methods including PayPal, Venmo, and Apple Pay to ensure the Home & School Club is collecting funds in the most convenient way for donors.

► Excelled in online courses including Accelerated Accounting and General Ledger best practices.

I once coached a woman who left the commercial workforce for five years to raise her son. As he was getting ready to go back to school, she wanted to move back into a fiscal specialist role at a university. She was previously a senior financial analyst at a prominent school and her resume was extensive. But for the past five years, she could only boast of sporadic volunteer work at her son's preschool.

We highlighted her overall skill set at the top of her resume (on page 136) using key words from job descriptions while keeping her volunteer activities shorter. The object is to "fill the gap" but not draw attention to it. The focus should be on the summary and where she gained the most relevant experience. Therefore, we categorized her previous role prior to leaving the workforce in a way that was easily readable, highlighting the key skill sets needed for the position she was applying for. We also combined the summary statement with the highlights section. Remember, there are no rules and every resume is unique![1]

The rest of her resume was on point and was also viewed through the lens of the new job. She applied for the job she wanted and remains there today!

Bold shows the key words that mirrored the job description.

First & Last Name
310-555-5555 • firstlast@gmail.com • Linkedin

ENTHUSIASTIC, DETAIL ORIENTED GRANT/CONTRACT MANAGER AND FISCAL SPECIALIST with a proven track record of

- **Pre- and post-award grant management,** including overseeing a **multimillion-dollar research portfolio** of **federal grants, industry-sponsored contracts, and endowments.**
- Performing **fiscal and administrative functions,** including **budget/proposal preparation, submission, financial reporting, payroll distribution, effort certification, internal audit, and year-end fiscal close out for all funding sources as well as purchasing, travel reimbursements, institutional compliance, and other essential research support functions.**
- Developing and implementing **best-practice policies and procedures for continuous improvement** and **providing education to stakeholders to ensure compliance.**

EXPERIENCE

Volunteer   2011–2019
JohnJohn Preschool, Jackson, FL

- Planned, promoted, and executed the annual silent auction including **managing and training** all volunteers and obtaining items for maximum revenue, raising more than $45,000 and exceeding previous year goal by 20%.
- Acted as liaison between diverse teachers, parents, volunteers, and school administration on simultaneous projects at multiple schools, while adhering to school guidelines, **state regulations,** and best practices for classroom management and **conflict resolution.**

Some people also take classes or get another or higher degree while raising children. Classes can be listed under the volunteer role or under education. They can be at a local community college, university, or online; you don't need to spend a fortune on a top-ranked school. If you achieve a higher degree while on a break, that should be listed under education. All education that helps you advance your career or keeps your skills fresh is helpful.

In a similar situation, a friend decided to leave an office job that she really enjoyed because she wanted more flexibility in raising her young children. She became a realtor for a few years and did some sales operations for the realtor company part-time. When she was ready to move back into a full-time job in sales operations, she asked me to look at her resume. The top of her original resume is below. Some of the dates/companies have been changed per her request.

First & Last Name

name@gmail.com • (555) 555-5555 • www.linkedin.com/in/name

Experienced sales operations professional focusing on pricing, project management, and people management. Strengths include creating and streamlining processes as well as hiring and managing highly effective teams that help the sales team to meet their sales objectives. Proven ability to think strategically; collaborate with cross-functional organizations; draft and implement sales operation processes; and develop and implement controls to monitor and improve sales operation processes.

Areas of expertise include:

- Establishing smoother operations management, allowing account executives to focus on selling.
- Managing cross-functional teams, including recruiting, training, managing, and developing resources.
- Implementing controls to monitor and improve sales operation processes.

EXPERIENCE

Company A, City, CA (part-time role)   2014–2020
Realtor and Sales Operations Manager
Joined an established team to streamline processes and workflow to increase business.

- Optimized lead management process and increased lead conversion rates.

- Consolidated disparate databases into a streamlined database and significantly improved client interaction and follow-up.
- Documented processes and improved workflow.
- Streamlined sales operations and marketing processes, including marketing campaigns and initiatives (web, print, client appreciation, and promotional activities).

Here is her revised resume based on the Sales Operations Manager job description; core job requirements are in **bold:**

First & Last Name
name@gmail.com ◆ (555) 555-5555 ◆ LinkedIn

SEASONED SALES OPERATIONS LEADER with expertise in sales analytics and reporting, CRM administration, sales compensation, Salesforce.com effectiveness, commercial contract management, and customer data management which support sales team goals.

EXPERTISE

◆ **Pricing Products**	◆ **Managing escalations**
◆ **Leading people**	◆ **Overseeing cross-functional projects**
◆ **Thinking strategically**	◆ **Implementing sales ops processes**
◆ **Optimizing processes**	◆ **Developing and implementing Deal Desk**

EXPERIENCE

Sales Operations Manager / Realtor   2014–2020
Company A, City, CA

- ◆ **Streamlining processes, creating efficient workflows, and optimizing lead management, including monitoring lead conversion vendors, establishing documentation protocol, and shortening lead response rate** by 75%, increasing **lead conversion rates** by 42%.

- **Restructured disparate databases** into a consolidated source of information, significantly improved client interaction and follow-up leading to 30% incremental sales.
- Create **analytics and reporting dashboards** to build visibility into the business and forecast challenges and opportunities.
- Manage real estate contract management and broker interaction to **fast-track closing of transactions.**
- **Streamlined sales operations and marketing processes,** including marketing campaigns and initiatives (web, print, client appreciation, and promotional activities) to attract new business and maintain contact with previous clients.

Her new resume was tailored to the job description for a specific job at a specific company and the rest of her resume was directly on point based on her previous sales operations experience. (You can find this entire resume example at https://www.marlolyonscoaching.com.). She applied for the role, received a phone call within forty-eight hours, and remains happily working and managing a team at that employer today.

Caring for a Sick Family Member or Yourself

This is noble and necessary, and if an employer faults you for this gap in your resume, that's not a company you want to work for anyway. Never say you were "stuck" caretaking. Own that you felt this was the most important job you could have in that moment and you were able to expand on your soft skills. How this person translated that experience when applying for a coordinator role is shown on page 140.

Someone applying for a finance job could discuss managing the trust or other financial affairs. Pick the areas in caregiving that are most relevant to the role you are applying to. The first bullet point talks about effective soft skills such as communicating and multitasking. The second bullet point talks about the same soft skills but also shows financial acumen.

Caretaker

Self-Employed (or Independent), City   2016–2019

- Effectively communicated with healthcare providers and coordinated meetings with healthcare professionals, financial institutions, and legal firms while caring for a sick family member, giving her peace of mind.
- Acted as executor of estate and worked successfully with multiple creditors, including credit card companies, utilities, medical facilities, and banking institutions to close out all financials quickly and efficiently.

Two bullet points are enough; keep it simple. Notice that the description doesn't say "caring for a sick grandmother in hospice." That's too much detail. Also, never write "Leave of Absence." Those are legal and HR trigger words that aren't always looked upon favorably. The object is to give enough information to fill the gap without too much detail to make it personal or awkward.

Traveling the World

All I can say is, bravo! How many people take the time to see the world? The experience most certainly schooled you on global mobility but also about different cultures. In today's global workforce, understanding other cultures is critical. Recruiters also say a person who has taken a sabbatical from the commercial workforce and traveled is ready to find that perfect fit when they start looking for a new role. You will likely find more jealousy that you took the time in the first place than roadblocks to reentry. Here is an example of how to position travel as both interesting and valuable:

World Traveler 2018–2019

Independent or Self-Employed, *worldwide (or region such as EMEA or APAC if you traveled regionally)*

- Traveled to 10 countries in APAC to understand how cultural diversity in the workplace impacts decision-making in business.
- Managed all travel visas and work documents and maintained immigration compliance records for smooth entry into every country.
- Gained written understanding and verbal fluency in Mandarin and Japanese.

If you traveled the world and worked odd jobs, you could use the above example or change the job title to Entrepreneur and add a bullet point (in **bold**):

Entrepreneur 2018–2019

Various Companies, *APAC*

- Traveled to 10 countries in APAC to understand how cultural diversity in the workplace impacts decision-making in business.
- **Worked in various roles including consulting on software-based start-ups, providing tours, and teaching written and verbal English communication skills.**
- Gained written understanding and verbal fluency in Mandarin and Japanese.
- Managed all travel visas and work documents and maintained immigration compliance records for smooth entry into every country.

Going Back to School

If you decided to take time off to go back to school and you interned or did real world school projects outside the classroom, use those as experience.

For example, picture someone who took two years off work to achieve her master's degree in Supply Chain Management. She wanted to use all her MBA projects on her resume, so she set up a "Doing Business As" (dba) consultancy through the local county clerk.

She did accomplish everything on her resume (see page 142) even though they were school projects. Also, some companies ask about projects as part of the interview process. If you do a comprehensive project (which I don't recommend unless you are paid as a consultant), then consider it part of your consulting work.

CK Consulting

Supply Chain Consultant, *Location*   2020–Current

- Design business strategies and translate into effective operations to drive both growth and profitability of a science and technology company, increasing revenues by 8%.
- Research and propose best practices to lower logistics costs, better forecast demand, and optimize supply chain integration for a transportation company.
- Determine best tools to provide accurate, real-time data and data analytic capabilities for a manufacturing company, reducing costs by 10%.

Employment Termination (Voluntary/Involuntary)

Have you seen the movie *Up in the Air* (2009)? It's based on the same-named novel by Walter Kim about Ryan Bingham, a "career transition counselor" who lives his life out of a suitcase, traveling around the country firing people. In the movie, George Clooney plays the Bingham character, and in a poignant scene, he is firing Bob (J. K. Simmons):

Ryan   *You know why kids love athletes?*

Bob   *I don't know. 'Cause they screw lingerie models.*

Ryan   *No, that's why we love athletes. Kids love athletes because they follow their dreams.*

Bob   *Well, I can't dunk.*

Ryan   *No, but you can cook.*

Bob   *What are you talking about?*

Ryan   *Your resume says that you minored in French culinary arts. Most students, they work on the fryer at KFC. But you bussed tables at Il Picador to support yourself. Then you get out of college and then you come to work here. How much did they first pay you to give up on your dreams?*

Bob   *Twenty-seven grand a year.*

Ryan   *And when were you gonna stop and come back and do what makes you happy?*

Bob   *Good questions.*

Ryan   *I see guys who work at the same company for their entire lives, guys exactly like you. They clock in, they clock out, and they never have a moment of happiness. You have an opportunity here, Bob. This is a rebirth.*

That's reportedly exactly what happened to Cozy Bailey,[2] who appeared in the film after she answered an ad looking for real unemployed people. She had more recently worked as a production tech at Dow Chemical. Before that, she was a line worker at DaimlerChrysler. At Dow, she only had the job for 18 months when she was laid off. With 19 years' industry experience, she thought for sure she'd get back in the business, but after three hundred resumes, nothing. So she started working at her friend's landscaping business and, voila! A new career was born. Now, more than a decade later, she has made yet another change and was recently elected as the Mayor of St Clair, Missouri![3]

Don't get me wrong. Having your employment terminated is never easy. I remember being let go from a job and feeling embarrassed because I didn't know how to explain it to potential new employers. I wasn't changing careers at the time; I just needed to get back in to get out *on my terms.* Understanding how terminations work and what it means to future employers will help take some of the edge off the "f" word—c'mon, I mean fired.

You may have noticed that when you are involuntarily terminated (aka fired), you probably aren't told exactly why. Maybe it "wasn't a good fit" or you weren't meeting expectations or some other generic explanation. Most companies won't go into details about the reason because they don't want to give you anything you can use to sue the company. Further, the decision is final anyway, so there's no point in starting a dialogue that could turn into an argument about specific reasons. A reputable company usually has a "very good" reason, so if you do sue, it will refer to its documentation of what your manager believed to be your lack of performance in either hard or soft skills.

That said, once you have left and are interviewing for new roles, most employers only confirm dates of employment and the title of your previous role. Big companies don't seek this information themselves; they hire a background check company to confirm it. Further, your previous employer likely won't answer the phone to provide such information, so many potential employers use a "hotline number" that is connected to their HRIS (Human Resources Information System) or payroll administrator.

To be clear, most background check companies use a third-party system and merely report dates and title. Therefore, the only way a new employer can find out if you were fired and why, is if the recruiter, hiring manager, or someone on the team you want to work for has a close friend or colleague at your old job willing to share why you left. So while you should never lie on your resume or in an interview about why you left a company, you may be able to express a different perspective (if you have one).

For example, when my employment was terminated from WDTN-TV, my first reaction was, "My boss is a jerk!" But I knew that wouldn't work when talking to a new employer. I wasn't very self-aware back then, so I couldn't see how I contributed to my exit even if my opinion at the time was confirmed by my colleagues that the boss was a jerk. That said, within days of my departure, it was announced that the station was being sold. I was now able to tell a prospective employer that my contract wasn't renewed during a station sale. I didn't lie; my contract wasn't renewed, and the station was being sold. That may not have been the *actual* reason my employment was terminated, but it was true. I presented it like this on my resume:

WDTN-TV

Reporter, Dayton, Ohio   1994–1996

▶ Reported, wrote, edited, and presented general assignment stories for air until contract wasn't renewed during a station sale.

When applying for new jobs, there were a few I definitely missed out on because the hiring managers at the prospective stations knew the news director at my old station. There was nothing I could write on my resume to give me a chance to talk to the recruiter and explain that this termination was eye-opening, that it made me look inside myself and how I could improve from a hard and soft skills perspective. Industries are small and people know each other, so I had to just keep trying to find the next role. A few weeks later, some contacts helped me secure a freelance role in Connecticut. That gave me a chance to show how much I had grown and provided me with new references, which led to a full-time position at a new station.

Whether you were involuntarily or voluntarily terminated, you should have only accurate information on your resume, including an end date on a job if you are no longer working there. The end date is the last day being paid through payroll, even if you were let go at an earlier date but kept on payroll for a period of time as part of your severance package. While most companies will fire you if they find out you lied on your resume, there are extreme cases of people going to jail. It was widely reported that Veronica Hilda Theriault was convicted of deception, dishonesty, and abuse of a public office when she fabricated her employment experience and education to obtain a chief information officer role with South Australia's Department of the Premier and Cabinet.[4] She was sentenced to 25 months in jail!

While that seems extreme, it is, at the very least, unethical to lie on your resume about where you worked, where you went to school, and what you've accomplished in your career. Some people who lied on their resume have ruined their careers. In 2006, David Edmondson was forced to resign as CEO of Radio Shack[5] after the company discovered he had no college degree, though his resume showed he had two of them. Wayne Simmons was fired from being a Fox News commentator and "terrorism analyst" and then immediately arrested after claiming to be a former CIA agent, which had helped him obtain government security clearances.[6] He was sentenced to 33 months in prison after he pled guilty to major fraud against the U.S., wire fraud, and a felony for illegally possessing a firearm.

Scare you enough? Good. Don't lie. That said, it's not unethical to position your accomplishments in a way to make them directly relevant to the role you are applying for. If you were fired from your last role or a previous one, it's fine to provide your perspective on your departure. Company reorg? Consolidation? Family obligations? Went back to school? Sometimes it is simply "a bad fit." And when you are terminated, it ultimately does boil down to that: fit. For whatever reason, you were unable to adapt or create the value the company needed at the time. If you say it was no longer the right fit, reference changes in the company strategy or boss or expectations for the role—perspectives that a potential employer will understand.

Chapter 10 Summary

1. **Own the gap:** Make sure you address time gaps in your resume whether you were a stay-at-home parent, voluntarily took time off for any reason, or your employment was terminated.

2. **Hone the narrative:** Determine your perspective on the gap and be able to confidently explain the reason in one or two sentences. Don't let the recruiter create the narrative.

3. **Don't lie:** Understand the difference between your "perspective" and a lie. Never lie about your experience or fill the gap with work you didn't do.

11

Tell a Great Story in Your Cover Letter

"Storytelling is the calculated release of information."

—Alex Garland, English writer and filmmaker

When is the last time someone told you a great story about a friend and you sat there riveted, wanting to know more and more about that person? You asked questions and were insatiably curious about every detail of how he or she either overcame a horrific experience or celebrated a great triumph. This is what your cover letter should be designed to do, connect the dots to make recruiters and hiring mangers curious about you.

First, let's be real. Recruiters rarely read cover letters and hiring managers rarely even see them. They are sometimes separated from the resume in ATSs, and most hiring managers don't even know where to find them. Further, many tech companies don't even have a place to type or upload one. But if there is a place to upload or type a cover letter, should you do so? It depends.

Tip #11: Cover letters are meant to tell a great story.

Don't write one if . . .

→ your resume and LinkedIn profile are complete, you are fully qualified for the job, and you are applying for the exact same job in a similar industry.

→ you aren't a good writer and have no one to help you. The cover letter could be your first impression, and a badly written one—especially with grammatical errors—could make recruiters not want to screen you.

Do write one if . . .

→ the ATS or company requires a cover letter to submit the whole application.

→ you are transitioning to a new career or new industry.

→ your resume has gaps that you were unable to fill on your resume or your resume doesn't tell the whole story about you.

→ you are applying to a company that is collecting resumes via email or other non-ATS channels.

Your cover letter can also be used as your introductory email to a recruiter if you are reaching out directly. Further, since you won't know if an application requires a cover letter until you start applying online, it's a good idea to have one ready.

What Is Your Story?

While there are no strict rules for writing cover letters, this chapter will cover some of the basics. Simple cover letters should be three to four paragraphs at most, with two to three sentences in each paragraph.

Paragraph 1: Start with a catchy first line that isn't too "cutesy," then mention the job you are applying for and the skills you have that will make you a great fit for this position.

Sentence 1: Catch your reader with your first words. If you want someone to read your cover letter (assuming they even open it), your first few words should catch them.

The best example is when someone refers you, because referrals will always get you in the door faster than a random application. First line examples:

Someone referred you:
Product Manager John Smith referred me to the [name of role] because he believes I would be a great addition to [company name].

Lawyer:

> My friends think I'm way too nice to be a hardcore negotiator. That's my strategy.

Analyst:

> If you were to analyze me, you would need to gather facts, so let me give you the basics about who I am and why I'm perfect for [company name] Business Analyst position.

Human Resources:

> Listen. That is the number one thing I will do to build relationships and coach the senior leaders at [company name].

If you're worried about coming up with something unique that doesn't sound silly, approach the first line in a more traditional way:

Traditional:

> It is with great enthusiasm that I submit my application to [name of role] at [company name].

or

> Please accept my application for the [name of role] at [company name].

Sentence 2: State what role you are applying to and some information about you that makes you a great fit. "A, B, and C" in the examples below represent three things from the job description that match your experience.

Examples:

> My stellar track record of [A, B, and C] in a global organization makes me a standout candidate for this role.

or

> My experience in [A, B, and C] makes me a strong candidate for [company name/position].

Another way to go is to rely on your resume and introduce your cover letter as having something new:

> My rich experience, knowledge, and strengths are outlined on my resume and LinkedIn profile, so I will take this opportunity to explain how my skills directly translate to this position and why I am the perfect fit for [company name].

Paragraph 2: Show lingo and set your story. What experiences in your life or on your resume make you more unique or more qualified than any other candidate? If you are career transitioning, this is where you apply the lens of the new job.

For a lawyer or a strategic business leader transferring to HR, look at similarities in your current role through the HR lens, which you can determine from the job description. Then determine how your current role allows you to bring a unique perspective to the HR role compared to every other HR leader with 20+ years' experience (**bold** for job description words):

> All managers need to be great leaders, but pressures, priorities, and people sometimes get in the way. I understand how the pressure to grow a business and the priorities that consume a day may leave little time to focus on people and their growth. **But people are the greatest asset for any company.** My deep experience in driving a business will allow me to bring a unique perspective to senior executives regarding leadership, people management, and development **to align people's skills with the companies' priorities.**

The last sentence highlights how the applicant's business experience directly relates to HR's entire purpose: aligning people's skills with company goals. Another example of a person in sales wanting to transfer skills to a diversity and inclusion role (**bold** for job description words):

> Leaders drive strategic initiatives through effective influence and advocacy. Every strategic initiative I champion is rooted in diversity

of thought through others' backgrounds, histories, and perspectives. My ability to **develop insights, identify gaps to inform strategy, and analyze and report out on metrics** that measure progress and effectiveness of each program from a **diversity and inclusion perspective** has **influenced senior leadership to review talent management processes, including performance management, compensation, internal mobility, engagement, and retention.**

Another way to translate skills in a cover letter is to focus on soft skills with specific words from the job descriptions. This example could work for nearly any career transition:

Remember when you were a kid and couldn't wait for your birthday to open all those presents? Every problem that needs a solution is like a present to me. Whether it is a **business problem, an employee capability issue, or a conflict among teams,** I'm the person who is excited to **align stakeholders** in finding the **best solution.** That is what makes me a great **leader:** someone who inspires and expects the same level of commitment from my team and the leaders I support in an always dynamic, **fast-paced environment.**

Paragraph 3 (optional): Example. Back up Paragraph 2 with a relevant and short story in three to four sentences that explain the exact work you are doing in the capacity of the new role without being in the new role.

As one of my employees was finishing her MBA with a concentration in data science, it was clear she had **gained skills** that could be valuable to the company but not fully utilized in my department. I provided her some analytics projects but she clearly wanted to **stretch her skill set** into a more technical area. As sad as it was to lose such a stellar employee in my department, I championed her move into the Data Science department where her **skills could best benefit the company.**

The above shows that the writer thinks about the value to the company and understands capabilities to benefit the company. For the sales leader who wants to transition to a diversity and inclusion role:

> When I provided **metrics** showing our sales leadership was not as
> **diverse** as other sales departments in similarly situated companies
> in our industry and uncovered that we don't recruit from **tradition-
> ally diverse (BIPOC) universities and colleges for internships and
> entry level roles,** my data **influenced** the CEO to mandate at least
> one diverse candidate must be interviewed for every role open at the
> company. Further, HR leaders looked at **promotion data** and asked me
> to help create specific **internal mobility guidelines** for all employees
> and **provide expertise in the formation of affinity groups** to focus on
> **engagement, retention, and education**. This effort opened communi-
> cation between diverse communities and senior leadership, resulting
> in a 20% increase in **diverse promotions** and **reduced turnover** of
> diverse employees by 16% over the past two years.

While there is a chance the above information is a bullet point on
your resume, it won't be nearly as complete as the above story, showing
influence, capability, and impact.

Paragraph 4: The close. (If you choose not to put in an example, then
this is Paragraph 3). The finish should be simple, no more than two sentences, emphasizing your desire to discuss your qualifications further:

> I hope I have persuaded you to see how my skills would make me a
> valuable asset in this exciting role at [company name] . I welcome
> the opportunity to meet with you about the position.

Putting it all together. Here is the actual cover letter I used when I
applied to Roku for the Director, HR Business Partner role—my first job
in HR. You'll notice, I took the more traditional approach (**bold** for job
description words):

> With a stellar record of **people management and development,
> identifying critical business needs, and implementing new
> approaches and programs to improve operational effectiveness
> to align with business strategy,** it is with excitement that I submit

my resume for your consideration for Roku's Director, Human Resources G&A role. My diverse experience as a **strategic business leader** in a **decentralized and matrixed global media organization** makes me a standout candidate for this position.

My rich experience, knowledge, and strengths are outlined on my resume and LinkedIn profile, so I will take this opportunity to explain how my skills directly translate to this position and why I am the perfect fit for Roku. I have spent more than 15 years in **media and entertainment** providing **strategic guidance to employees,** from assistants to division presidents, in areas including **organizational effectiveness, talent growth, learning and development, and change management.** I not only understand, but my track record shows, **excellence in implementing modern HR principles to engage employees, starting with recruiting, and continuing through employees' growth with the company.**

To highlight one success story: As one of my employees was finishing her MBA with a concentration in data science, it was clear she had **gained skills** that could be valuable to the company but could not be fully utilized in my department. While I provided her some analytics projects, she clearly wanted to **stretch her skill set** into the more technical area. As sad as it was to lose such a stellar employee in my department, I championed her move into the Data Science department where her **skills could best benefit the company.**

My passion for people and how they **contribute to business success,** combined with my **global reach, business acumen, and emotional intelligence in coaching,** makes me a stellar candidate for your Director, Human Resources role. I hope I have persuaded you to understand how my skills would make me a valuable asset in this role.

I welcome the opportunity to meet with you about the position.

Best,

Marlo Lyons

Notice, though, that I never said, "While I haven't worked in HR . . ." During my interview, I was asked many times if I was in HR and I always answered very directly, "No, but . . . ," continuing to explain the skills I possessed that were directly relatable. And, the cover letter told a story, positioning all my skills through the perspective of the new job. In the above example, you see the positioning is about employee retention and aligning people skills with company goals.

I wrote the recruiter a message through LinkedIn after I applied online:

> Hi Bob,
>
> I'm reaching out to you to directly express my excitement about the Director, Human Resources G&A role at Roku, Inc. My extensive experience in entertainment combined with my legal history and specific strategic experience would make me a tremendous asset to Roku in this role. I hope you will seriously consider me for this position and give me an opportunity to explain further how I can bring outside-the-box value to the company.
>
> Thank you!
>
> Marlo

He responded and we set up time to talk on the phone. While Bob told me he didn't read the cover letter until after we chatted for the first time, he did leverage some of the information to convince the hiring manager, the head of HR, to talk to me.

Another way to approach a cover letter is to cover your soft skills while explaining your experience. The trick is to not repeat your resume. Here is the cover letter the financial analyst who wanted to return to the commercial workforce used to secure her new role:

> With a stellar track record of grant management and financial administration, it is with great enthusiasm that I submit my resume for your consideration for [role]. My experience, knowledge and strengths outlined on my resume makes me a standout candidate for this position.

During my three years at [last company name], I provided strategic expertise to the CAO and a large research development team on all aspects of administrative, fiscal, extramural, and departmental funding. My strong work ethic, ability to learn, dependability, people skills, and meticulous attention to detail were instrumental in helping to secure a multimillion-dollar research portfolio for [last company name].

My focus every day was to deliver results through positive and efficient communication, prioritization, and organization. While I have taken some time away from working as a senior financial analyst, I am a life-long learner and have continued to hone my skills through taking financial accounting courses. Now I am ready to jump back in and bring my skills to [company name].

I hope I have persuaded you to understand how my skills would make me a valuable asset in this exciting role in [company department]. I welcome the opportunity to meet with you about the position.

A couple final tips of what not to write in cover letters:

1. **"I."** Don't start every sentence with "I." Find other ways such as with "My."

2. **Don't copy/paste.** Cover letters are not meant to reiterate your resume; that's why you have a resume. Cover letters are meant to enhance what's on your resume with soft skill descriptions and how your skills will transfer easily to the current role.

3. **Research for tone.** How do you know whether to go with a fun or traditional route in your cover letter if you haven't worked at the company? Start with the internet. Look for how the company describes its culture. Easygoing? Fast-paced? Is the company big or small? You will also pick up clues from the way a company describes itself in its various communications and "About Us" documents.

4. **Don't get personal.** Don't talk about your kids or husband, wife, girlfriend, boyfriend, significant other, etc.

5. **It's not about you.** Don't talk about what the role will teach you or what you hope to learn. Cover letters are about *the value you bring to the company*.

6. **Proper grammar/punctuation.** The same advice for resumes goes for cover letters. Write in complete sentences with proper grammar. If you don't know how to use a semicolon, learn before using one. If you aren't a good writer, have someone read it for you before sending it. This could be the first, second, or third impression a hiring manager has of you. If they like you after reviewing your resume and then read a poorly written cover letter, it will give that recruiter serious pause as to whether to keep advocating your candidacy.

Chapter 11 Summary

1. **What is your story?** Write down two or three stories that relate your current job to the new job. Shorten the story to four sentences or less.

2. **Paragraph 1:** Introduce yourself with a catchy or a traditional opening that explains who you are, who referred you (if applicable), what role you are applying for, and how your skills are perfect for the role.

3. **Paragraph 2 (and 3 if needed):** Tell a good story that incorporates hard/soft skills that are directly relatable to the role based on the job description.

4. **Paragraph 4:** This is a closing statement requesting a chance to further explain the value you can bring to the company.

12

Leverage LinkedIn

"Your LinkedIn profile should leave no room for doubt about the kind of job you're looking for and why you're the best person for that position."

—Melanie Pinola, *LinkedIn in 30 Minutes*

Back when I was applying for my first job, I had a Brother word processor, fancy stationery, fancy matching envelopes, and stamps. That was the only way to apply for jobs. Resumes were photocopied or printed onto nice paper and sent out one by one with cover letters. Then you would wait to hear something, anything. Today we have LinkedIn, the single most important asset for a job hunter as well as the single most important asset in networking. Quite frankly, LinkedIn is your greatest asset when it comes to finding a new job, transitioning to a new career, or meeting people in your industry or other industries. And it's the best way for people to find you.

At any given moment, approximately 30 million companies have pages on LinkedIn. That means 30 million companies regularly use LinkedIn to source people for employment. In fact, at any given moment, 20 million jobs and 90,000 schools are listed on LinkedIn worldwide. There is no better place to find the job of your dreams than LinkedIn. And there is no better place for recruiters to find you

Tip #12: Leverage LinkedIn (and other social media) to make it easy for recruiters to find you.

than on LinkedIn. In fact, many recruiters have told me they are skeptical about an applicant's experience if they don't have a LinkedIn profile. The only type of person who may not be able to post a LinkedIn profile is someone with high governmental security clearance who could lose that clearance by having a social media presence.

Once you have a LinkedIn profile, recruiters should be reaching out to you proactively without you even needing to apply for jobs. Recruiters say the number one way they find candidates is by doing a Boolean search with key words from the job description on LinkedIn. Therefore, if you aren't hearing from recruiters, it's because your profile either isn't as complete as it could be or you haven't positioned yourself properly for the jobs/career you want to move into. So how do you get recruiters to find you? You leverage every field on LinkedIn.

Filling in LinkedIn Fields

1. Personal photo: The number one thing people look at on LinkedIn is your profile picture. In fact, LinkedIn reports profile pictures get 21 times more profile views than profiles without pictures. Your picture should be you, alone, from the shoulders up, dressed in professional clothes against a neutral, plain, and simple background setting. You aren't outside in the woods (unless you are a forest ranger or looking to be a bike tour guide) and you aren't standing in front of a distracting background. You don't wear a prom dress or a wedding tux no matter how stunning you look because that's not for a work environment. Your picture is also not a fraternity or yearbook picture, which is a bit too professionally stiff. And it is not you in a group shot.

How do you get such a perfect picture? Most people have cell phones and know how to take a nice picture. Dress nice, put on makeup if applicable, do your hair, and stand in a neutral location but not too close to a wall where you will have a shadow. Consider having your hair or makeup professionally done at the mall or at a store like Sephora or any makeup counter in a department store like Macy's. That's how I was able to secure a professional photo.

I was invited to an event at the local mall that offered a "makeup make-over" and up to 15 professional photos on a zip drive if I bought $75 worth of product. I needed some product anyway, so I thought, *Why not?* I had my hair professionally blow-dried before the event and gave clear instructions to the makeup artist to keep the makeup subtle for a professional headshot. At least six other women were doing the same! These types of events happen all the time. All you have to do (if you wear makeup) is check the makeup counters at stores like Bare Naked, Mac, or Sephora to see if a particular brand has any upcoming events or visit the brand's website.

The picture on the back cover of this book is the picture I have on LinkedIn today—simple and professional. It is also only four years old, so I can't promise that by the time you read this book I haven't updated it. Sure, I have a few more wrinkles than when it was taken but it still looks like me. I know this because at least once a year I check with colleagues who know me to make sure!

Rule of thumb: Update your picture every five years or if your appearance has changed dramatically (e.g., you had long hair and now it is pixie short) or you lost or gained weight in your face. LinkedIn isn't a dating site, but your picture should look like you or an interviewer might question your integrity or self-esteem.

My last piece of advice is to smile or at least have an approachable expression. Smiling makes you look inviting and warm and suggests that you don't take yourself too seriously. It should make someone want to get to know you, even have lunch with you! In the interviewing section, I will explore how to convey that warmth in conversation.

2. Background photo. It's not critical to change the stock photo that's there, but if you have a background photo that is more inviting, add it. Be careful not to pick one that is too busy or distracting. Simple colors / simple message is best. Further, make sure the photo works on mobile devices.

3. Headline. The headline under your name will be pulled from your most current job but you can edit it. Pick a headline that conveys who you are and what experience you have as you define yourself in your new career. Mine says, **"Executive Coach / Career Strategist / Business Partner / Author / Inspirational Public Speaker."** I do speak publicly but not too often—yet. I'm an author of articles but this is my first book. What I am conveying is who I perceive myself to be and how I'm showing myself to the world. This is my story and how I define *me*. Use this headline along with your transferable experiences to define yourself in your new career.

4. Summary. The summary section is just that—a short snippet of who you are. This is the same summary you put at the top of your resume, so it's okay to "copy/paste." If you are applying for various kinds of jobs, then use a more generic or a broader summary on your profile. After the summary statement, consider adding your "Expertise," "Highlights," or a short list of "Achievements." If you have this section on your resume, use some of those words and/or phrases in the profile. Bullet-point each one and make sure there are key words from job descriptions in each as long as those key words are applicable to your experience. This section should not only reflect your experience but also your personality if you are able to showcase that.

5. Experience. LinkedIn states that profiles with completely filled-in experiences are ten times more likely to get messages to and responses from recruiters. Experience on LinkedIn, if positioned properly with words from descriptions of the jobs you want, should attract recruiters through their searches. It is critical to be as clear on LinkedIn as you are on your resume, but LinkedIn is not meant to be your resume. It is meant to entice an employer with highlights about who you are and what you have accomplished.

I am asked all the time, "Should I copy my resume onto LinkedIn?" You can and that is fine. You can also shorten or elongate what you put on LinkedIn. If you choose to copy/paste from your resume, you will have bullet points on LinkedIn; otherwise, there is no bullet point option. Some people would rather put short paragraphs under the job title instead of bullet points. That is fine, too, if it's only two or three sentences with active verbs and includes an overview of your experience that includes key words from a summary of the job descriptions of the job you want. Most recruiters and hiring managers don't read long paragraphs. The most important thing is to make sure your overall LinkedIn experience timeline matches the timeline on your resume. If it doesn't match, recruiters will consider that a red flag.

6. Education: Education is meant to give a high-level overview of your accomplishments and where you went to school. It is not a place to list every award received or activity you participated in. Your most recent degree should be listed first. If you have an MBA and a bachelor's, the MBA goes first. You don't have to add the actual dates you entered and finished your education or your GPA unless you want to. What matters is that you achieved the degree. Further, most companies don't care about GPA unless you just graduated. If you think the years will help you because the hiring manager went to the same school or you have a GPA of over 3.5, then feel free to include it.

If you have any specific activities that are relevant to the role, include them under "Education." For example, if you haven't been working in marketing but are trying to transition to a marketing role and were the president of the school's marketing club and brought in big-name speakers, include a sentence on the knowledge/experience gained that shows you have some skills in marketing. For example:

President, Marketing Club
- Brought in chief marketing officers from [company names] to educate the membership about different marketing practices such as brand, product, communications, public relations, and sales and the difference between working at an agency versus working in-house at a company.

If you went to school more than ten years ago and have been working since, activities become less relevant, but it doesn't hurt to briefly include them. If you are looking for a legal job and you have been published in

a law review (e.g., an article or note), include those under "Education."
If you are the first one in your family to graduate college or graduated at
the top of your class while working full-time, list that. It will make for a
good talking point. Here is how mine looks and I've been out of school
more than ten years:

Oklahoma City University School of Law

JD, Rank #2 / Magna Cum Laude   1999–2002

Activities and Societies: *Law Review*, Phi Delta Phi Legal Honor
Society, writer for *The Verdict*

Attended OKCU night law school while working full time as a
television news reporter and graduated in 3 1/2 years; ranked #2.
(I just couldn't beat that guy Paul—he was SMART! Thank goodness
I was smart enough to make him my study partner.)

- Published Note: "Switching Stations: The battle over non-compete
  agreements in the broadcasting industry."? 2002
- Covered U.S. Supreme Court Hearing for KWTV / Published
  Comment: "Earls ex rel. Earls v. Board of Education: Violating the
  Fourth Amendment's Spirit."

The George Washington University

BA, Political Communication

A few explanations about the above: I did add the year of my graduation for law school but not for undergrad. Why? I earned that degree in
1991 with a 3.4 GPA. That's a long time ago and makes me "old" in some
employers' minds. And while I was proud of my GPA, a 3.4 doesn't mean
much decades later. For law school, I wanted to show that I have had a
legal mind since 2002. For those employers who like to do math and
think I went to law school right after graduating college, they will believe
I am eight years younger than I am. Their fault, not mine. (Shame on
them for trying to do the math!)

And while no one really cares what I did 25+ years ago, the *Law Review* and legal honor society convey that I am smart, while *The Verdict* shows I am a writer. Former lawyers who may now be hiring managers know that being published is a great accomplishment. While none of this is relevant to my current role in HR, over the years it has become apparent that these published articles are interesting talking points with recruiters and hiring managers. Remember when I said there is no right or wrong? If it feels right or conveys an important message about who you are, put it in.

Notice the two sentences that humorously describe the overlap between school and work. In this case, in stating I went to law school at night while working full-time, I was trying to convey my ability to successfully multitask. That is not just a skill in and of itself but will resonate with a lot of hiring managers who have conquered night or weekend college or graduate school while working full-time. It's also part of my "story" when I talk about my transition from TV news to working in entertainment. As for Paul, I should thank him because he not only taught me a lot when we were in school, but he has become quite the talking point with recruiters and given me an opportunity to show my personality a bit. Thanks, Paul!

7. Licenses and certifications: Make sure you include all of these, especially if the license or certification is relevant to the role. My law degree is not entirely relevant, but it shows I made it through law school and have a legal mind no matter what career I choose. And while I don't practice traditional law, I sometimes use my degree to interpret new laws that affect employees or to conduct employee investigations. So, it does have relevance and that's why I keep my license active. Put all such achievements in order of relevance. My coaching certification and SPHR and GPHR are listed above the law license.

8. Volunteer experience: Include it here, not on your resume unless your volunteer experience is the only directly relevant experience you have to the new role. It makes you human and tells a little more about you as a person than what your work history reveals. Write a short paragraph (two or three sentences) about what you did, what the organization does, and the impact that volunteering had on you and/or the people you were helping. "I" is fine to use in this section as long as most of the messaging is about the organization.

9. Skills and endorsements: Hopefully, you have some endorsements in your current career. If not, whether looking for a job in the same career or transitioning to a new one, endorsements can be powerful. If you have some of the relevant skills for a new career, add them to your "Skills" section so your colleagues can endorse you. For example, I was coaching a lot in my previous job even though it wasn't in my previous career's job description. After I added coaching to my skills list, I asked anyone who had experienced my coaching to please endorse me. LinkedIn also allows you to pin the top three to be seen at a glance on your profile. When recruiters do a Boolean search, these skills could help you be found. Since most recruiters won't open the tab to see all your skills, make sure the top three are directly relevant to the career you are seeking. Don't ignore this section. Skills endorsements can draw attention and should be optimized.

10. Recommendations: This section is critical. How do you get recommendations? If you've been working for a while, figure out who the hiring manager would want to see a recommendation from and/or who would be the most valuable recommendation for your new career. If applying for an HR role, you'd seek out the "head of people" or someone in Compensation or Learning and Development. For a Government Affairs position, it may be nice to hear from a lobbyist or politician you influenced. In the legal world, you would want to hear from a general counsel or colleague more senior to your level. It is always helpful to have a former boss's recommendation or someone you worked with cross-functionally. If you don't know people in the field, then it's impossible to get a reference from them, which means you'll have to tap into your network to get one. I also recommend sending the people who agree to write a recommendation for you a few topics or bullet points of what you'd like them to cover. Otherwise, they could all sound the same. For example:

Hi Jon,

Thank you so much for agreeing to write a recommendation for me on LinkedIn. As you know, I'm applying for roles in the marketing field. I'd appreciate it if you would cover my ability to work in a chaotic, fast-paced environment and my ability to adapt to change. Also, if you can connect my work with marketing, that would be ideal. Remember when we worked together on that bakery project? That would be a good example if you need one.

Thank you again,

[your name]

Whether the recommendation is from your current job or a previous one, always make sure the reference knows to relate your current work to the job you want. For example, Brenda Madden is a colleague from my reporting days. Reporting and HR have very few similarities, so I asked her to write a recommendation that covered my professional presence, communication and interpersonal skills, work ethic, and ability to multitask under extreme pressure and deadlines. She wrote the following:

Marlo and I worked together as reporters in Dayton, Ohio. Since then, I have watched her become a rising star in the corporate world. Her exceptional interpersonal and communication skills, combined with a professional presence developed from years of on-air reporting, have always allowed her to stand out among her colleagues. As a reporter, your job is to convince people to talk to you on camera during the most stressful times of their lives. It also requires you to find creative solutions to meet the needs of multiple people—producers, editors, photographers, the news director, and, of course, the viewer. Marlo's unique ability to do that often led to coveted assignments, including overseas travel to Israel and numerous high-profile stories. Those skills also prepared Marlo for her success today.

As an attorney, she manages multiple priorities simultaneously and possesses a work ethic that would rival even the most accomplished CEO. But the quality that makes her a true asset is her ability to care. As a journalist, she cared about every person she met and every story she told. As a co-worker, she cared about the success and well-being of her colleagues. Her drive to excel made her a leader in our newsroom, the type of employee who motivates everyone to do their best, so it's not surprising that she continues to be a driving force to this day.

This is the strongest recommendation in that section because she wrote about me as a human being within the context of my work. This allows people to know me better without having to talk to me. Having someone write about your soft skills is even more important than your hard skills, especially as you mature in your career. If your colleagues aren't good writers, write your own recommendation as an example or send bullet points and ask them to edit it in their voice based on what they want to say.

11. Follow Industry Organizations and Groups Are you following industry groups so you will see articles by them? Look for state, regional, and national industry groups that are relevant to the career you want to move into. Follow companies that you want to work for or that interest you. You will see articles by these groups that may help with lingo, contacts, and understanding the new career. Following industry groups also shows you are serious about the new career.

What *Not* to Put on your LinkedIn Profile

→ **Your grades.** Your school grades are irrelevant. Multiple headlines suggest many millionaires were not the best students.[1] Grades are not indicative of your success in the workplace.

→ **Your hobbies.** If you like to ski, great! Cook? Fantastic! Save it for Facebook, Instagram, or other social media platforms.

LinkedIn is for professional posts only and your profile should exemplify that.

→ **"I" or "My."** Just like your resume, do not use "I" or "My" on your profile unless you are writing about your volunteering activities.

→ **Name-dropping just to name-drop.** Name-drop only if it matters. If you are a talent agent or lawyer who works with A-list clients and you have permission, go ahead and drop a few. It shows you aren't intimidated by stars. It also suggests that you can deal with difficult personalities and that you have experience with higher-level deal-making. But only name-drop if there is obvious strategic value because the risk is it could turn off a recruiter or hiring manager.

→ **Confidential or proprietary information.** LinkedIn is not a place to post anything that might be seen as confidential to the company you worked for. For example, many companies don't disclose their client lists or the projects they work on. Further, government employees have dozens of confidential projects and listing even the names of the projects could be an issue. If you only work on confidential projects, cover your employment history broadly with the skills used to be successful in that career instead of the names of projects or companies that benefited from your work.

Check Your LinkedIn Settings

Once your profile is as complete as it can be, make sure the "backend settings" are what you want. Click on your small picture/"Me" icon on the toolbar, review each of the settings, and decide which ones make the most sense. Two key settings are the following:

→ Under "How others see your profile and network information," click on "Edit your public profile" and choose "Public" so you can be found.

→ Under "Job Seeking Preferences," make sure you click on "Let recruiters know you're open to opportunities." Generally speaking, LinkedIn tries to prevent people from your own company from seeing you are "open" to new opportunities, but there are no guarantees. I have always clicked this open-opportunity button when I'm looking for a new job, and the last time I did, I asked a recruiter from my company if I appeared "open." She said no, so I felt confident enough no one at my current company would see I was "open" but recruiters outside my company would be able to see it. If you want recruiters to find you, make it easy for recruiters to know by choosing the right settings.

Other Social Media

LinkedIn is not the only place to build a profile or to communicate your experience. You can post your resume for free on Monster.com, Indeed.com, CareerBuilder.com, ZipRecruiter, Glassdoor, Craigslist, TheMuse, and USAjobs.gov. Your local college may also have a job- or resume-posting site. Finally, associations or organizations are a great place to post your resume and make connections. There are hundreds of them, and some are specific. For example, the American Association of Blacks in Energy (AABE) was developed to provide thought leadership in the development of energy policies and regulations, emerging technologies, and environmental issues. On AABE's website, members who work in the energy industry can post resumes and search for jobs. Whatever field you are interested in, Google the subject and association for an opportunity to not only post your resume but to network!

Chapter 12 Summary

1. **Leverage LinkedIn:** Use this powerful networking and candidate-searching tool to the fullest extent.

2. **Picture:** Take a head-and-shoulders picture in front of a solid background.

3. **Summary:** Include a statement of who you are and any specific expertise or skills in this important section.

4. **Experience:** Copy/paste your work history from your resume. Add more detail with key words as necessary.

5. **Education:** Include activities and publications if timely and relevant.

6. **Licenses and certifications:** List the most relevant ones first.

7. **Skills endorsements:** Ask colleagues to endorse the relevant skills needed for the new career.

8. **Volunteer activities:** Use this section to humanize your profile, showing your personality and the causes you are interested in.

9. **Recommendations:** Ask a minimum of three colleagues to write recommendations that describe your hard and soft skills and tie your current or past work to your new career.

10. **Follow organizations:** Find at least five organizations that are relevant to the new career and follow them.

11. **Other social media:** Don't just rely on LinkedIn. While most recruiters will find you here, posting your resume on other career, association, or college websites will allow you to network and also be found by hiring managers who have similar interests.

13

Interviewing: The Recruiter Screen

"I sometimes find that in interviews you learn more about yourself than the person learned about you."

—William Shatner, actor, author

YES! A recruiter reaches out to you via LinkedIn, email, or phone and would love to set a time to talk. Your response to that inquiry and your chat with the recruiter will create the very first personal impression beyond your resume and LinkedIn profile. Think about that—the very first personal impression. And yet, recruiters report that some candidates take that first phone call in the grocery store line, on a city street with sirens blaring or while they are chewing gum or eating lunch (chomp, chomp). None of these locations or situations are okay! Candidates have also answered the phone with, "Yo, John here" or "Hello? Is this a scammer?" or simply "Hello." Then the recruiter identifies him/herself and the person says, "Who?" Recruiters can only think, "Seriously?" These screens should be taken more seriously than the hiring manager interview because you won't get to the hiring manager if you don't pass the recruiter screen.

Tip #13: The recruiter will determine whether you have the hard and soft skills to fit the role and the company during the initial screen.

Respond to Every Recruiter Call

If the recruiter asks you for a time to chat, set a time where you will be in a quiet place with a good phone or internet signal. If you know you have a day full of back-to-back meetings, don't "fit in" the call between meetings. Find a day, time, and place to speak where you can compose yourself a half-hour before the scheduled call. Even if you have to wait a week before you get such an opening, the recruiter will likely still want to speak to you, but if other candidates are in play, there's a chance you may miss the window. Simply put, you won't be presented to a hiring manager if you *don't* make a good impression on the recruiter, so it's worth it to wait if necessary.

Your timely response to an initial recruiter contact is just as important as subsequent calls because the recruiter will gauge your interest by how fast you first respond. If you are working full-time while applying for jobs, check your voicemail, LinkedIn messages, and personal email multiple times a day. (Even if you are not actively looking, keep your antenna out.) Also, your response needs to be clear and concise and free of grammatical errors. The recruiter is not your friend, so responding back with, "Hey, sounds great" or using abbreviations like this will raise a red flag: "I'd love to hear about the role but I have an EMBM tomorrow so I'm not available until Friday. It would be easier to chat not DWH." (That's "early morning business meeting" and "during work hours" for those who aren't familiar.) Even if you would never work for the company the recruiter is contacting you about or the role is the same level or uninteresting, set up the call and use the time to impress the recruiter with who you are. Remember, recruiters move and get hired to recruit for new roles and new companies every day. Also, you never know when an opportunity you never thought would interest you does pops up.

A close friend and colleague of mine, Samantha, had been working at a major entertainment company as a lawyer for five years. She loved her job and the people around her including her boss. It had all the flexibility she needed with two small children at home. She could walk to work and even go home to have lunch with her kids. She had no intention of leaving and thought she'd eventually take her boss's job when he retired. But one thing was missing: VP stripes. It wasn't about the title; it was about a title that was commensurate to her experience that would also set her up as his successor. Then LinkedIn sent her an ad for a coveted position at a leading tech company. She applied online and a company recruiter called her a few hours later! She thought maybe she'd use an offer as leverage to be promoted to VP in her current role, but the more she talked to the recruiters and hiring managers, the more intrigued she became. In addition to the same flexibility, she found more pay, better benefits, and a presumably great manager (she hoped!). By the end of the process, the tech company had won her over and she's still there today. That great manager worked out!

Research the Recruiter

Once you've scheduled a time to talk to a recruiter, prepare for the screening interview by researching the recruiter. Yes! Research the recruiter! Is it an internal or external recruiter? An executive recruiter? What types of candidates does the recruiter seek? Learn who the recruiter is and what they specialize in. Also check to see if you have any mutual connections on LinkedIn. If the recruiter asks about one of them, be prepared with an answer, such as how well you know "John" or that it's a random connection based on mutual respect for each other's career and experience in the field.

Research the Potential Job

If the recruiter told you the name of the company or the job title, find the job description that will be posted on the company's website and/or on LinkedIn and research the company. Sometimes the recruiter will attach the job description to the initial email or give a link. Other times, the recruiter may send you an email that talks about an exciting and unique opportunity along with a job title but doesn't give you the company name or any more information. The goal is to tease you to gauge your interest. For example, I once received this LinkedIn message:

> My team is working with a global independent entertainment studio on a VP HR role in LA. In this role you will be responsible for driving the organization's people plan in support of the overall business strategy

with an emphasis on tasks including workforce planning, organizational change execution, management effectiveness coaching, performance management, etc. I looked through your profile here and I think that your background and experience are extremely relevant. If this has piqued your interest, simply let me know that you'd like to learn more.

Within 15 minutes, I figured out it was Entertainment One. How? I searched for posted VP HR roles in Los Angeles and there were five—one at Entertainment One, described as a "global independent entertainment studio." I was then able to research Entertainment One so when the recruiter mentioned the company, I was able to say, "Yes, I'm familiar with the company. I believe it produced *Private Eyes*, which I enjoyed, and I know its family brand is very strong with *Peppa Pig* and *PJ Masks*, two of our family favorites." Being able to confidently discuss the company and industry landscape automatically created a connection with the recruiter.

What to Expect in the Recruiter Call

From researching the recruiter, company, and role, you can establish your strategy on what theme or message you want to leave with the recruiter and how your experience would be valuable to the company he or she is representing. The recruiter screen usually lasts between 30 and 60 minutes and has four purposes:

1. Explain the role and company to you. If the recruiter didn't send you information on the specific job or company and you haven't been able to figure it out yourself, this is the time to learn! There is no expectation that you have done any research. That said, if the recruiter did send you information on the job or company and you have done your research, there is still more to learn about the role. The job description never covers every aspect of the job. For example, recruiters meet with hiring managers to discuss the intangibles, which are either described on the screening call or the recruiter will ask questions to detect if you have them. Intangibles can mean the hiring manager wants someone with a background as a product manager even though it is a business development role. Or the manager is looking for an entrepreneurial background or will only talk to people who were innovators in first-generation technology. Think of job descriptions as a large net trying to haul in the obvious candidates but also some, like you, who are out of the box with unique experience to bring to the role.

2. Make sure you have the hard skills. The job description is a wish list of hard and soft skills that the ideal candidate should possess. The recruiter will have discussed with the hiring manager which hard skills are absolute "musts" or foundational to the role and which are not as important. Reminder, hard skills are the actual skills needed for the role such as Salesforce proficiency, SQL expertise, or specific writing skills. Most of that is covered on your resume or LinkedIn profile, so the recruiter is just confirming that you have the experience you say you have (they may ask for examples) so they can check off those boxes.

3. Gauge your soft skills. As you answer questions about your hard skills, recruiters are gauging your soft skills. Some soft skills that relate to the workplace are people management, cognitive flexibility, decision-making, influencing, learning quickly, working outside of structured processes, working cross-functionally, interpersonal skills, and being solution oriented. As you answer questions about projects and accomplishments, did you describe how you influenced leaders in decision-making? Is your tone appropriate while you are talking? Do you seem either arrogant or too humble as you describe your accomplishments? Are you impatient with the questions? Do you talk in circles but never get to the point? Do you think you're having a nice debate but you are really argumentative on an issue? How you discuss your qualifications matters.

For example, one person asked me, "Please describe the steps you took to introduce a big change to a group or company." Before I worked in HR and early in my interviewing process, I described how I rolled out a safety program at Viacom by working with outside counsel, drafting required documents, and presenting the program at roll-out meetings. One recruiter asked me, "Was the program easily adopted?" That's when I realized my story was leaving out the most important parts of the answer: the soft skills I used to accomplish the goal and what I learned from the adoption process. For example, I'd left out the stakeholder management piece—preflighting the information to get buy-in and influencing those who would be responsible for program compliance, which would be a lot more work. Showing you learned something from a project shows self-awareness, which is a key skill for any job. So try to fit some soft skills into every answer about hard skills.

4. Determine whether you are a culture fit. The recruiter will listen to how you discuss your experience to assess whether you will be a culture fit within a company. Are you quiet? Loud? Too energetic? Enjoy working late? It may be okay to be all these things or none of them depending on the unique culture of the company. There is no point in putting you through the full interview process at a company if the recruiter knows the fit would be wrong.

Merriam-Webster describes culture as "the set of shared attitudes, values, goals, and practices that characterizes an institution or organization." A simpler description: "Culture is a way of being within a company."[1] For example, some cultures may require consensus before a decision is made, while others listen to all ideas but the decision-maker has unilateral authority even if the decision is the opposite of what the majority believes is right. If you are interviewing for a company where you could be overruled even though your idea is the best, the recruiter will probe if you can handle that or whether it will frustrate you. Or if you worked at a large company where all the processes are already in place and you are applying to a start-up, you may be asked if you are comfortable with a lot of change, chaos, and loosely defined swim lanes on projects.

Netflix has an especially unique culture that it lays it out for candidates on its website.[2] It describes employees working on a "Dream Team" where everyone is extraordinary at what they do as well as highly effective collaborators. No one at Netflix is coasting or what some call "resting and vesting." Low-performing employees are routinely terminated. The Netflix website essentially admits it: "Many people value job security very highly and would prefer to work at companies whose orientation is more about stability, seniority, and working around inconsistent employee effectiveness." That pretty much says, perform if you want to stay. Slackers should not apply. Roku had a similar cultural identity, calling it a "sports team" (not a "family," as some do). The line I heard most often was, "You don't pay your family to work with you and perform." A sports team requires that everyone bring consistent excellence or risk being kicked off the team (demoted to a lower league, cut, waived, contract not renewed) "Kicked off the team," in HR speak, means fired.

Amazon has a similar culture but also a specific way of holding meetings, where Jeff Bezos has reportedly banned PowerPoint presentations.[3] Instead, they've been replaced with a detailed six-page memo that must be read by everyone in the meeting before it can start. Bezos/Amazon believes that memos provide deeper clarity on an issue and create more effective communication. It can take a week or more to draft a memo and numerous people may edit it. Recruiters for Amazon thus screen applicants for their ability to embrace Amazon's mission and strategy as well as its unique communication style and a candidate's ability to draft a memo that fits the culture. Amazon's culture is so unique, there are dozens of blogs and even a course about how to prepare for an interview.[4]

Culture may also include how fast a company moves in making decisions, how much work each person is expected to accomplish, and whether employees are expected to answer emails after normal working hours or on weekends. At Roku, the pace was intense and incredibly fast. Most people were emailing and working before they arrived at the office and long after they left in the evening. They would also text and email on weekends. I thrived in that fast-paced environment, but it also felt like a treadmill that at times I wanted to get off.

By comparison, the very first thing I noticed about the culture at Intuitive was that I rarely received emails at night or on weekends. I would check my phone over and over—even restart it to make sure the Outlook app was working—before I realized the culture didn't require nonstop communication. There was certainly a lot of work to do, but you were expected to spend uninterrupted quality time with your family when you were home. Moving to a role at Intuitive meant more time being 100% focused on my kids in off-work hours, not half-focused on them while trying to keep up with the needs of the business. It was a hard adjustment for me after working at such a frenzied pace for the previous decade. Now, we all know COVID-19 has changed the meaning of "work-life" balance, especially if you have kids. With much of the workforce working from home, it may have also changed some companies' cultures.

While you can understand pieces of a company's culture by asking about it, there is no way to absorb all the nuances until you live it. I asked about culture during my Intuitive interview and was told that the people were really nice, the leaders were smart, and everyone believes in the company's mission. Every interviewer pointed to the leadership and individual expectations framed on the wall and said that employees truly live by those. It all sounded rewarding and purpose driven. Some of the leaders asked why I'd want to leave Roku, which had to be more exciting than "boring med-tech." They had alluded to the company's products being in a highly regulated industry but also emphasized how much work there was to do, so I didn't quite grasp how different work would be at the new company. I even called a few friends of friends who worked there, and from all the questions I asked, and information provided, I still didn't know I'd have mostly free nights and weekends. Adapting to this "quieter" job was a blessing and yet also a struggle. In fact, my boss said her biggest concern was my ability to adapt. She almost didn't hire me because culture is harder to teach than hard skills. Fortunately, I figured out how to still be "me" while adapting to a slower pace. Then the pace picked up and I realized it really wasn't that slow at all. The culture wants you to take time to learn first before jumping in, and I fully jumped into the crazy busy stage about a year into the job. But my nights and weekends still remain mostly free!

There is nothing worse for a recruiter or hiring manager than realizing that a new hire has the perfect experience and will drive business but that certain aspects of their personality or how they conduct business are antithetical to the company culture. Sometimes a new hire will realize that something is wrong but can't figure out what. At other times, they perform as they always have but don't receive direct feedback of what isn't working and so they continue to alienate co-workers or customers.

It's not the "what" a new employee is doing but the "how." That is why recruiter screens are keenly focused on culture fit.

Prepare Answers to These Five Questions

Instead of seeing recruiters as gatekeepers, think of them as the experts who know whether you will be successful in a role. From that first phone call, the recruiter will know whether to sell you or not even mention you to the hiring manager for the next interview stage; your fate is in their hands. Being prepared for this screen and presenting yourself in the most favorable and accurate light is critical. How will they determine if you are a right fit? They will ask what seem like introductory or innocuous questions, but how you answer these five questions are key to whether you are a culture fit:

1. Tell me a little about yourself? This question unnerves nearly everyone. Do you talk about your career history? Do you walk through your resume? How about your hobbies? What does a recruiter want to hear when asking you this question? Essentially, they want to get to know you. They want to get a feel for your energy, level of authority, whether you are super serious or can be personable with a light joke. They want to understand how you think and if you "get it," meaning you have emotional intelligence. They want to get to the heart of YOU and what's important to you so the recruiter can determine if you will fit the company culture, with the team, and in the role. They also want to know what you aspire to do. How you answer this question will set the tone for the rest of the conversation.

Substantively, this question is not asking about your equestrian adventures or your last ski trip but at the same time it is asking exactly that. What makes you *you*? What makes you tick? What are your values? What is important to you in the workplace and life? You've already done a values exercise (see Chapter 2), so you have a roadmap for what to emphasize. For example, are you a voracious reader? Do you love learning and/or teaching others? Are you the person everyone comes to when they need to solve a problem or someone to talk to who will listen? Do you like to mentor and coach people? Are you good at letting things roll off your back and not get rattled under pressure? Determine the soft skills you have that connect with what is important to you. For example, consider someone who loves to read:

> When I think about my career and life, the one constant is that I'm a voracious reader. I read pretty much everything I can get my hands on and that has really served me well in learning new areas quickly. I have transitioned careers a number of times to a field I knew nothing about, but reading, talking to people, asking smart questions, and listening have allowed me to learn anything I don't know but need to know.

In answering this one question, the candidate has already shown an ability to learn, to listen, and to adapt. Another example is someone who loves to travel and is applying for a global role that will require travel to a company's offices in the Asia Pacific:

> I am a lifelong traveler. Learning about new cultures is important to me, and the best way to learn about them is to travel. My last adventure was to Japan, which is an interesting country from a social hierarchy standpoint. It's similar to India in that reputation and manners influence how to work successfully in those countries.

By answering the question with a little bit of knowledge about Japan and India, the candidate shows an understanding of cultural differences and how those impact a workplace. For the person who wants to address the issue of why they are interested less than two years into a new job:

> I have been extremely fortunate to have worked for some amazing managers and incredible companies. I have learned over the years that the best work environment for me is one that fosters independence, isn't political, and has strong leaders who make decisions quickly after discussion. I also discovered that it is hard to find such a great environment. I have heard that your company would match my values, and that is why I was so interested in talking with you today.

Cultural insight, whether gained in distant lands or in the U.S., is applicable to every job. That said, you may also have a unique personal history that enhances the conversation.

Alissa from The Winford Group says that some of her most memorable candidates had unusual backgrounds, from running a marathon backward to an obsession with the *New York Times* crossword puzzle. What makes them memorable? "They simply stood out," she said. "I can't tell you anything about people I meet who are serious, bland, and nice because they are forgettable." She advises finding the one thing that makes you interesting and memorable. "We can't all be writers or Olympic athletes, but we can stand out in some unique way, and when there are hundreds of resumes in the pile, that matters."

Don't confuse standing out with getting overly personal. Don't bring up your family, medical illnesses, hardships, or anything negative. Also know that this question is Part 1 of the "story of you." How you answer it, plus the energy and vibe behind it, will either entice the recruiter to want to hear more or end the call early. No pressure!

2. Can you walk me through your resume? This sounds like an easy one to answer, but it's not. You should be able to walk a recruiter through your resume in less than two minutes even if you have worked for 30 years or had 15 jobs. Recruiters are not asking you to talk about everything you did in each job or even talk about each job. They want to hear the highlights of your applicable skills in a story, incorporating how you transitioned from job to job. In talking about each role, they want you to connect the dots about what you've done, what you've learned, and how your experience and knowledge will bring value to the role you are interviewing for. They also want to know the reasons behind any gaps on your resume, no matter how small.

Start with your first job. Your story starts with your first job after college or high school, if you didn't go to college. The only time you would talk about college is if you are the first in your family to attend one or if there is some other unique fact such as being the first in five generations to attend a different school than the rest of your family or your passion for your chosen career began in a specific class (e.g., a passion for marketing began in a subliminal messaging class). Still, any conversation about college should be in one to two sentences. For the most part, you will start the conversation with your first job or, if you have been working for 20 years, a summary of the "type" of jobs you had early in your career.

For example, a marketing professional who started her career in advertising sales in three different jobs more than 15 years ago wouldn't discuss each sales job and what she learned but would say something like, "I started my career in advertising sales and that was a great foundation for the roles I've held since then because I was able to hone a pitch and learn how to effectively influence people in a large, matrixed organization." That's a lot of substantive information in just one sentence! It summarizes the role she had, the skills she gained, and how she used them in a large company across departments. Work on creating a bold statement for each job and how that job connects to the role you are applying to without using obvious words such as "and that is similar to the role I'm applying to." When describing the roles you've already had, make sure to reference some core concepts from the description of the job you are applying for. Here is how I describe my varied experience (**bold** highlights key words in the job description and parentheses tell you what I am trying to convey with each statement):

As you can see, I started my career as a TV news reporter. That's where I learned how to **hustle on tight deadlines nightly and hone my written and verbal communication skills,** and where I built my **executive presence** (I can speak to executives). When the internet was taking off, I realized TV news wasn't going to be the only source of news, so I went to night law school while working full-time as a consumer-investigative reporter (hard worker/multi-tasker). After graduation, I moved to LA to be a screenwriter. We both know how that worked out (humor). That's when I landed a media and legal risk assessment role at NBC, where I vetted reality show participants by reading their background checks and psychological and medical evaluations. You might call it a "psychological profiler" (creating intrigue). That was the beginning of my passion for **understanding people on a deeper level—how they would react on set, after the show taped but before it aired, and then after it aired** (HR—understanding people).

A former colleague at NBC moved to Viacom and recommended me (I'm good!) for a role there that was broader in scope and responsibility and included **immigration and crew mobility** around the world as well as child labor compliance and managing overall safety on our sets (upgraded role/understanding of HR functions). When my husband took a job in the Bay area, Viacom asked me to stay on (I'm worth it!). I did so for a year and then tried to figure out what I could do with all these skills.

Through the suggestion of a recruiter and a lot of research, I chose HR Business Partner (new career wasn't a whim but calculated) because I was most successful at NBC and Viacom **strategically helping leaders create successful TV programs by understanding people, which in essence is helping leaders build strong teams of people with the right skills to drive a business and manage people-related issues as they come up on set** (HR skills). I realized I should get certified in HR to prove I understood the nuances of HR, so I took and passed the **SPHR and GPHR** and also spent a full year getting certified in executive **coaching** (HR understanding/spent time in coaching, not a quick pay for the certificate scam). While I coached a lot in my NBC and Viacom roles, I wanted more tools in my toolkit and I love to learn, so it made sense to complete this certification (capacity to learn).

That is nearly 30+ years of work told organically in story form in less than two minutes. Notice that I didn't talk about any one specific accomplishment from my resume. I covered my work history broadly and related it to the role I was applying for (HR Business Partner) with key words from the job description (in **bold**) in a story form. In my last three jobs,

I had specific stories or examples of how I brought value to each role in a way that is consistent with the new career. While I had this script in front of me, it was critical that I did not sound like I was reading! After saying it enough, I no longer needed notes. It was my story. Uncover the parts of *your* story that will add intrigue and personality so the recruiter can get to know you. Your friends know you best; ask them what makes you interesting!

Also notice the transition between jobs. Recruiters want to know the details of what made you leave each role. As you move through your resume from the oldest job to your most recent, discuss why you made the move from one job to another. Did you apply? Were you poached? Were you fired? Transitions are important, especially if you were recruited because it infers your value: If you were "stolen" from another workplace, that means you have a good reputation. If a former colleague or manager poached you, say it! That shows they valued you enough to want to bring you with them into their new company. As shown above, my transition statement from NBC to Viacom includes, "A former colleague at NBC moved to Viacom and recommended me for the role . . ." I never worked directly for that colleague, but he was instrumental in me being hired since I didn't initially apply for the role. Giving context for each move builds your credibility.

This is also the time to explain gaps in your resume. Whether you wanted a change, had family obligations, or needed clarity of mind to decide your next move, explain what you did while you weren't in the commercial workforce. Did the time off help you gain clarity? Motivate you to find the right next move? Help you hone new skills to make you a better employee?

While it's never a great idea to say you were fired, there are some exceptions that allow for transparency such as being terminated during a mass layoff, a job elimination during a reorganization, a change in management, or the company shuts down. Most recruiters understand that such things can happen. But what if you were fired for some other reason and you don't know why? While you might feel "tainted," if you were planning to change careers and the termination helped make that transition a reality, position your departure through a positive perspective. Here are some generic examples:

> I realized after ten years with the company that I needed to take a break from the 80-hour work weeks to invest in me and figure out how to leverage my skills in this new area. I knew it was a risk to walk away from a successful career, but I also knew it was necessary to make this transition.

or

> I always wanted to work in [field], but as long as I was employed, I would never have made the leap. Walking away from a successful career as a [title] put the right amount of pressure on me to truly go after what I want for my future and bring value to the right organization.

or

> After my tenth trip around the world for work, I realized I was missing valuable time with my family, so I decided to take some time off and reevaluate my career. The role here at [company name] is exactly what I'm looking for and where I know I can bring the most value.

While any of the above positioning *could* be true, your positioning may be questioned if someone at the company you are applying to has a relationship with someone from your old company and can find out that you were fired (even if they can't find out why). If recruiters can't get exact information about a departure, they may ask a former colleague if they'd work with you again. Even if you know why you were fired, it will be hard to show you have learned from the experience if you are unemployed and/or haven't worked since. When I was let go from WDTN-TV and started looking for new roles, I heard that news directors from the stations I was applying to were calling colleagues and the former news director I worked with at WDTN. I remember being a finalist in two jobs and losing them overnight. When that happens, you just have to let them go and look for the next opportunity.

If you *are* currently employed, were fired earlier in your career, and know there are mutual connections who could derail you being hired in a new role, be transparent and explain how that experience helped you grow. Showing self-awareness of your flaws and failures from an old job can help keep you in play for the new position. An example would be:

> I was fired from [company name] because, well, I was pretty angry back then about a personal situation and not nearly as self-aware as I am now about how my anger was affecting me and others at work. I went through an anger management course and really practiced those skills. I'm actually glad I had that experience because it gave me an opportunity to grow and change. Now, nothing really riles me up, and one of my strengths on all my reviews is my ability to influence effectively in the toughest of circumstances.

or

> I was fired because I was an alcoholic. Yes, I was. I'm three years sober now and couldn't be happier with my life and the achievements I've been able to accomplish since that really difficult time.

This level of transparency will automatically tell the recruiter you are self-aware and honest, which will quickly build credibility and trust. Some recruiters, however, may be put off by such honesty and decide you aren't "perfect" for the role. Further, one area you don't want to bring up is a recurring mental health issue such as PTSD, anxiety, or stress because no matter how much you've recovered or improved or received help, recruiters will not be able gauge whether the same issues will surface at the new company.

It's your goal to own your perspective on why YOU left any particular company, not why someone caused you to leave. Your manager may have fired you for a lack of hard or soft skills, lack of urgency, or any other reason. Your perspective may be that you had a horrible boss, you were caught up in politics, or had a lack of clarity from stakeholders to be successful. While you can't say any of those perspectives without looking like a complainer, find the perspective for the quick transitions between jobs or job gap that shows you have grown from the past role, especially if you don't think the prospective employer has any connections to that old job. An example:

> I realized early on the role I had taken was not as it was described to me. I still wanted to give it a shot and I did for the time I was there. But ultimately, I realized it wasn't a right fit for me and the skills that make me most successful couldn't be utilized to the fullest based on the maturity of the company. It was a great learning experience that is allowing me to look much closer at the next opportunity to make sure I am in sync with the company and hiring manager.

I'm not suggesting that you lie but recognize that some people won't believe that someone can change or grow without telling the recruiter what you learned from the previous experience. You will want the recruiter to understand that your moves were as positive as possible.

3. Why do you want to leave your current company? Why did you leave your most recent company? Why are you looking? If you haven't already answered these types of questions while walking a recruiter through your resume, be prepared to succinctly address them. Every article about employee attrition and employee engagement will tell you that people leave jobs because they hate their manager or there is no room for growth. It is no great secret. But it is not a good idea to mention anything negative about your manager because it might suggest to a recruiter that you couldn't find a way to build a productive relationship. Any negativity could open the door for the recruiter to wonder if you are the problem and not your manager.

If you've been at a company for a long time, or you didn't get the raise/promotion you wanted, or your manager has limited your growth potential, you can say, "I'm looking for a new challenge at the next level" or "I'm at the top of my game and comfortable in my current role but there is no way to keep growing here based on the structure so I am looking for the next opportunity that makes me a little uncomfortable." If you are contacted by a recruiter but you aren't necessarily looking, you can simply say, "I am not actively looking but keep me in mind because I don't want to miss out on an exciting opportunity." If you are transitioning careers, don't just say, "I want to be in X field." You'll want to explain the transition steps you've taken to convince a hiring manager that you are serious about the new career. The more steps, the more serious you will look.

Whenever I mentioned that in some ways I was already taking on HR responsibilities without being in HR and looking to move into a traditional HR Business Partner role, most recruiters asked how I knew that's what I wanted to do. I gave a detailed explanation:

> As you can tell, I've had numerous careers, and after we moved to the Bay area, I wasn't sure what I wanted to do. So I went to a career coach and started talking to people about my current skill set. I realized that the parts of my current job—coaching, advising, dealing with sticky people situations that have no playbook—are directly transferrable to an HR Business Partner role. I decided to learn more about it so I studied the field and took the SPHR and the GPHR. I also coached a lot in my job but realized there must be more to coaching, so I took classes and obtained my certification after 500 hours of training, instruction, and practice. I am now ready to transition into this new role.

The most important thing to do is connect the dots of how current or past roles relate to the role you want to move into. You can see in my explanation above that I talked about "coaching, advising, and dealing with sticky people situations that have no playbook," all of which are core skills as listed in HR Business Partner job descriptions.

4. What interests you about the role at [company name]? Research. Research. Research. You must do research on a company before taking a recruiter call. You are expected to know enough about the company to sound knowledgeable and to show you put effort into checking it out. I suggest the bare minimum research include the following:

1. Public or private?

2. Who is the CEO? What was their trajectory? Who is the leader of the department you'd be working in and what was their trajectory?

3. How many people are in the company?

4. Is the company domestic or worldwide? Where are its offices?

5. What service or product does the company provide?

6. What is the company's Glassdoor rating (be sure to read through the comments)?

7. Read about company culture.

8. Leader or disruptor in its field? Competitive environment?

9. What makes the company unique compared to others in the space?

10. Do you have any relationships with people who work there? If your LinkedIn profile shows such a connection, the recruiter will ask how you know that person.

After doing your research, you should be excited to work at the company for specific reasons. For example:

[Company name] is a leader in its industry. It is disrupting the way we do [Y]. That type of drive to be number one and stay number one when the competition is fierce describes the company I excel at.

or

I've done some research on the company and talked to a lot of friends who work there (be prepared to name them if asked) and they all say its vision is solid, the culture is fantastic, and the leaders are strong. I'm looking for a company where I believe in the products and the people behind them and I see this role as perfect for my skill set.

or

I am looking for a company that is changing the world. I want to know that the work I do is going to help people in a profound way and Company X is innovative and doing just that.

The answer to what interests you about a company can be this simple. Don't say, "I have an Amazon Prime membership so it would be fun to work there!" Find a way to show you did your research. At the same time, don't go into detail about the company's products or how it brings in revenue unless the role is related to sales or finance. And while you can usually discover a lot about a company, you won't gain a full understanding of how it does business until you are on the inside.

5. What is your expectation for compensation? It may seem odd that a recruiter would ask this so early in the interview process, but the last purpose for the recruiter screen is to determine if you and the company are aligned on salary expectations. I have been asked this question during every single first recruiter conversation because if our numbers are too far apart, there is no reason to go forward. The most important thing is be ready to answer the question without stumbling. Recruiters in some states may ask about your current salary, but many states now have laws that forbid a recruiter from asking what you currently earn. From New York to California and numerous states in between, recruiters can no longer rely on salary information in making employment decisions or offers. The goal of these laws is to fix pay inequality.

An important aside: In 2019, the National Partnership for Women and Families found that women made 79 cents for every dollar earned compared to a white, non-Hispanic man for the same job regardless of seniority or job type. Further, people of color continue to experience a gender wage gap. Latinas are paid on average 54 cents and Native American women are paid typically 58 cents for every dollar paid to a white, non-Hispanic man. Black women—62 cents. So, if recruiters aren't supposed to ask about compensation, how can they still be asking this question? Because the question is about "expectations" and not actual salary information. As uncomfortable as the question is to so many, it's critical to answer it professionally.

If you provide a salary expectation that's too high, there's a chance a recruiter will decide you have priced yourself out of the role. If you provide one that's too low and you are offered that amount, you will kick yourself later and not feel valued and it may take years or moving to yet another new job to catch up, if ever. If you decide to ask for more after realizing your mistake, you could come off as untrustworthy or flakey and the negotiation will be much more uncomfortable. (See more about negotiating in Chapter 15.) Remember, the main purpose of the question is to determine if the company can afford you. Some recruiters will use salary to gauge your level of seniority in your current company. Here are some steps to consider when answering this question:

a. Determine the minimum you need to live. Figure out how much money you need to put food on the table, a roof over your head, cover essential needs, with some money for entertainment, babysitters, etc. Then determine what you think is a fair wage for your years of experience and the location of the role—a position in San Jose is going to pay a lot more than the same position in Oklahoma City because the cost of labor is much higher in San Jose. Come up with a number without doing any research so you have an idea of what you personally need and want.

b. Check salary aggregator websites. Research salaries on sites such as Salary.com, Payscale.com, Monster.com, Glassdoor, and Google Play's salary calculator. Look also at public data through the Bureau of Labor Statistics. Consider reviewing information on the Society for Human Resources Management (SHRM) website or job-specific compensation data from professional and industry associations. And you can always do an online search using the job title and the word "compensation." You'll be surprised at how much public data exists on salaries. Make sure you look at the right level for the role and whether it includes managing people or working as a nonmanaging employee. Cross-referencing is also critical. When I checked some of those sites, the salary differences were surprisingly broad—a lot lower or higher than what I'd been offered in the past. Still, from all this research, you will gain a fairly good idea of what to expect.

c. Talk to people. Talk to friends and colleagues in the same field or reach out to contacts you've made on LinkedIn, especially recruiters and those in HR. Ask what they think someone with your years of experience in another field, trying to break into a new field, should expect to earn. Any current manager knows the salary ranges of their employees; just don't ask a manager from the same company you are interviewing for as that would be a conflict of interest! Keep in mind, you may not break in at the same title level you currently have. I had to go from vice president at Viacom to director at Roku and from a legal pay scale to a nonlegal pay scale. And yet I was paid more at Roku than Viacom because I moved from entertainment to technology and I entered as a director. Know the level you need to enter and make sure you bolster your knowledge and resume to align at that level.

Now that you have all that information and you are fully prepared, do everything you can to not answer the question. You read that right. Do everything you can to answer the question without actually answering it. First, answer the question with a question: "Is there a range for the role?" In California, the company has a legal obligation to provide you the range. The recruiter might say, "I don't have that handy but will get it to you. What range are you hoping for?" You can politely state, "I'd love to hear the range and I'm happy to let you know if we are aligned." Or use one of my favorite lines: "My expectations are negotiable. I want to be fairly compensated for the value I'll bring to the role." If the recruiter provides you a range, you can answer with either "I was thinking the high end of that range is on target" or consider pushing a bit: "That range is slightly lower than what I was expecting but we're close enough that I would love to continue the conversation."

If the range proposed is way too low, try, "Wow, that is a lot lower than I expected." There were numerous jobs where the range wasn't even close to what I was looking for. Either the role was much more junior than what I wanted, or the company didn't value HR the way other companies did, or a particular industry paid lower than other industries, or the company was simply looking to get a Tesla for the price of a Toyota.

Usually there is some wiggle room in the range being offered since it is somewhat based on years of experience. Even if I didn't have years of HR experience, I was being considered for director-level work because the hiring manager believed in my transferrable skills; therefore, I should be paid at a director level. If pressed for an answer as to what your range is, you can respond with, "Right now my total compensation is X. In my next role, I am looking for a range closer to Z." What that says (without saying it out loud) is, "Don't dismiss me because my current salary is probably what you're offering, but I'm really looking for something more." I did that once and was told my range was closer to what they paid VPs and they would consider me for those roles as they came open. Other times you will simply be out of the range. If you researched the roles, levels, and salaries and you aren't asking for something far beyond what the market is paying, you need to re-evaluate whether this is the right company, industry, or job level for you.

Remember, some recruiters are comparing your resume and seniority with your expectations. Do they match? The number one thing you don't want to do is agree that the range provided is in sync with your expectations and then, when offered the role, ask for more. That is a waste of the recruiter's time and comes off as deceptive.

Although answering a recruiter's questions requires preparation, it is not just about what you say but how you say it. What answers are you most comfortable with and where do you stumble? Confident people don't stammer or over-explain or feel like they need to justify their career decisions. They don't get defensive if the recruiter asks additional questions to understand how a career choice was made. They own their decisions and explain their job moves, time off, and other choices with confidence. For example, in coaching stay-at-home parents and people who have taken a break from work on how to explain job gaps, I have found that while the words are there, the confidence and presence in presenting them are not. Such parents worry about justifying the time off or fear that employers will feel they aren't ambitious or career oriented.

Developing a strong sense of presence—knowing who you are and what you are about—will bring the confidence you need to own the decisions you have made in your life. In her book *Presence*, Amy Cuddy writes that presence "is the state of being attuned to and able to comfortably express our true thoughts, feelings, values, and potential."[5] The object is to defeat the thoughts and assumptions that make you feel powerless, thoughts like, "Who will hire me since I haven't worked in eight years?" or "I'll never get a job" or "What if I'm behind the times because I've been gone for so long?" Cuddy writes about how showing power on the outside can help people overcome how they feel on the inside. She describes "power poses" such as the Wonder Woman pose: hands on hips and your feet slightly apart. She writes, "Let your body tell you that you're powerful and deserving, and you become more present, enthusiastic, and authentically yourself." Stand up and try it. Feel more powerful? More confident? Use that power to answer those five typical interview questions in a way that convinces a recruiter that your career and life choices make you the best candidate for the role.

Be Curious with Questions

Finally, all recruiter screens should end with *you* asking questions. This is your opportunity to learn more about the company but keep your audience in mind. The recruiter has probably set aside 30 to 60 minutes to talk to you. Don't keep them on the phone needlessly even if it's the first recruiter to show interest in you. Ask one or two questions that a recruiter can answer. Don't ask detailed questions about the day-to-day responsibilities of the job itself because the recruiter likely doesn't know. Save those questions for the hiring manager. During a recruiter screen, consider simple closing questions such as:

→ "What makes people successful at [company name]?"

→ "I did some research on the culture, but can you describe how you see it?"

→ "What has the hiring manager said is the most important skill for this role?"

→ "What intangible skills are you looking for in this role?"

→ "Have you noticed the culture change since COVID-19?"

→ "Is there anything I have said today that concerns you or makes you feel I am not a perfect fit for this role?"

→ "What is the interview process like from here at [company name]?"

→ "I'm very interested in the role you described. If I'm fortunate enough to move to the next round, what is the process?"

By asking that last question, you will know where you are in the process if you receive a transparent answer. If you don't get past a recruiter screen, chalk it up to not being the right fit in hard or soft skills or in culture. Or the recruiter may sense you aren't being authentic. Recruiters don't want some mythical version of you—they want *you*. If you are selling yourself the entire time and not paying attention to where the conversation is heading or you can't turn off the "interview version" of you, the recruiter may pass before you get a chance to talk to the hiring manager. Therefore, answer each question with authenticity and showing some personality that will allow a recruiter to determine if you are truly a viable candidate for the role and the company.

Chapter 13 Summary

1. **Take every recruiter call:** Build a relationship with every recruiter because you never know if a recruiter will present you with an incredible opportunity now or in the future.

2. **Research the recruiter:** Know if you are you talking to an internal or external recruiter or executive recruiter and the kind of company that is interested in you.

3. **Know the purpose of the recruiter screen:** A recruiter's screen is meant to explain the role, describe the company, make sure you have the foundational hard/soft skills for the role, determine whether you are a culture fit for the company, and understand your overall interest in the role by the end of the conversation.

4. **Prepare answers to the typical five questions:** Write down two-minute answers to the five questions recruiters usually ask using key words from the job description that directly connect your current role to the career you want to be doing.

5. **Exude confidence:** Be confident in your answers; practice before every call.

14

Beyond the Recruiter Screen

"Before anything else, preparation is the key to success."

—Alexander Graham Bell, inventor, scientist

If you didn't make it through the recruiter screen, try to get feedback from the recruiter as to why. Most of the time you will receive the proverbial, "We had candidates who better matched what we were looking for." But if you've built a relationship with the recruiter and you take the rejection well, sometimes you'll get some useful feedback. Simply ask, "I understand there are a lot of great candidates out there. I am going to interview with other companies, so any feedback you can give on my interview with you would be most helpful." While many companies and recruiters are scared in this litigious society of being sued for discrimination for their feedback, they may still provide some insight that will explain their decision and help you in the future.

If you made it through the recruiter screen, celebrate! That is a huge accomplishment. But as they say, now the real work begins. You will win or lose the job over the next round of interviews.

No matter how much I try to make candidates feel comfortable while interviewing them in my role as a hiring manager, I know they aren't. There you are, sitting either in person or via video, in front of the person who is deciding during a 30- to 60-minute interview whether you have a future at their company. The more a candidate wants

Tip #14: Prepare, prepare, and prepare some more.

the job, the more uncomfortable some become. I have seen extroverts turn into introverts. I have seen people sweat, shake, and clasp their hands so tight their fingers turn red. Even I get nervous. I am pretty loud in general, which could be off-putting to some, but I'm also nervous in interviews that my bubbly personality almost becomes too stiff.

Fortunately, interviewing doesn't have to be horrible! In fact, most companies are fighting for the right candidates (especially during times of low unemployment), so if they are working hard to recruit you, you should work just as hard to gain their faith and show why you are the best candidate. And it doesn't matter if you are interviewing in person or via video. Via video, only two things change: the location and whether you can have notes in front of you.

Via video, make sure you have a well-lit location. Consider what is in your background. Is it warm and inviting? Will it make people feel uncomfortable? I suggest not having a bed or toilet in your background if at all possible. Also, a wall right behind you may cause you to cast a shadow. Adhere to the rule of thirds by positioning your head in the upper third and fill most of the screen with your shoulders. Don't show lower than your torso. When interviewing, if you are interrupted by a child, simply apologize once, or introduce your child, be kind in helping your child into another room, and let it go. During COVID-19, life and work has co-mingled and if an interviewer doesn't understand that, then it probably isn't a place you want to work anyway.

While interviewing via video may seem less personal, an advantage to interviewing from home is you can have notes. I would never recommend bringing notes to an in-person interview, but at home, no one can see if you have notes, as long as you don't sound like you are reading. If you get nervous and forget what you want to cover during interviews, consider taping a sheet of paper with a few short bullet points to the wall just past the camera lens. No matter where you are interviewing, the key is to listen carefully and answer the exact question being asked succinctly and thoroughly while showing some personality to help the interviewer understand if they would enjoy working with you every day.

Positioning Your Work

Resumes open doors; interviewing closes them. The question is, which side will you be on when they close? Thus, how you position your experience and skills is critical. But how can you do that if you don't know what they will ask? The good news is that you don't need to know the questions. You do need to prepare answers that will fit any and all questions asked. For example, here are five common interview questions from hiring managers:

→ "What accomplishment are you most proud of?"

→ "Tell me about a time when you've had to deal with a situation and knew you'd encounter resistance?"

→ "Tell me about a time when you were responsible for a work process innovation?"

→ "Tell me about a problem you had with a client and how you solved it?"

→ "What are your strengths and what areas do you need to develop (aka weaknesses)?

These seem like totally different questions, but you could handle them all with one answer if your greatest accomplishment was solving a business problem using innovation and getting buy-in from stakeholders before rolling it out. Here's how to do just that.

Step 1: Review the job description and think about all the big career accomplishments that stand out in your mind that **relate to the job description and the new job.** What makes your examples accomplishments? Did you complete a big project? Did you have to get stakeholder buy-in? Work cross-functionally with different groups? Influence different people? Learn a new culture to show global understanding? Now, take five big accomplishments that are directly applicable to the job description and prepare five different examples of your work using the STAR method.

Reminder: The STAR method is Situation, Task, Action, Result. **Situation** is the "what"—the challenge or business problem that needed to be solved. It is best to present a challenge you identified or found yourself in and you were charged with coming up with the solution. Don't describe a situation that someone else was in and you came in and "saved the day." Those examples may be viable but describing them may come off as arrogant if not positioned well. **Task** describes the goal or what you needed to achieve. When will you know a solution is in place and working? **Action** is the "how" you did the work to bring about the solution and reach the goal. This is the perfect spot to describe soft skills. **Results** are the outcomes and measurement of those outcomes. Whenever possible add the T for Takeaways as well. By concluding with a takeaway, it shows growth and learning from the experience.

When discussing issues in the STAR method, it is important to use the word "I" even if you are describing a team project. It is fine to use "we" at times, but make sure the interviewer knows what you did specifically to solve the issue. Otherwise, the interviewer won't know if you personally brought strategic vision or value to develop the solution or if you were just part of the tactical executing team. Own what you did! Here is an example of an engineer who wants to move into marketing:

SITUATION: What business problem needed to be solved?

Problem: We had a product that wasn't moving off the shelves at the rate of other products and we weren't sure why. Was it not being marketed and positioned in a way to drive consumers to buy it? Or was it a competitive issue and it needed the right features for an emerging market?

TASK: What would help that **Situation** change and how did you come up with that?

The goal: Our goal was to increase sales by a minimum of 10% for this product and/or understand more deeply why this product wasn't selling as fast as our competitors' products in order to help business leaders revise their marketing/positioning strategies and/or help the engineering team enhance the product with better features.

ACTION: What actions did you take to change the **Situation** and in what order? Hold brainstorming meetings? Influence stakeholder buy-in? Collaborate closely with cross-functional co-workers? Bring in outside vendors? Did you motivate your team? Don't forget to include your soft skills here!

Actions taken: I conceived an out-of-the box marketing campaign we had never tried before. Since it hadn't been proven before, I worked hard to convince senior leadership that this was worth trying and used data to show how this campaign could drive an increase in sales of at least 10%. I also worked closely with our brand and strategy teams to create the strategy behind the campaign and convey the right vision. I knew the campaign needed to be measured, so I also worked closely with our market research and insights teams to create surveys and consumer studies to make sure we had the best research on our competitors' product. The campaign went live in just two months and included new creative for video, web assets, and social media.

RESULTS: What were the results of your efforts?

Measurable outcomes: Click-through data showed we sold 20% more during the campaign than the year before and 40% more than each month during the previous year. New product research also showed that if we had added one more feature, sales could have been even higher; previous research hadn't discovered that. Based on our success and this new data, I was able to then influence the R&D teams to change the roadmap and start building out that new feature.

The rollout likely didn't go as perfectly planned, which gives you a chance to show what you learned from the experience and what you would do differently next time. For example:

TAKEAWAYS: What did you learn and how did you grow from this experience?

Learnings/Change: The campaign was clearly successful, but had I stopped and taken the time to test that other feature, it could have been added relatively quickly and might have moved the needle even further. The takeaway for me is to make sure I keep my eye on the prize but to sometimes look sideways because you never know what you may find that could have an even greater impact.

With five examples crystalized in this format, nearly any question can be answered about your work experience. Try to incorporate both hard and soft skills in each example and use at least one example to focus on soft skills, specifically communication, influencing, time management, flexibility, or trust. This will reveal your ability to juggle multiple projects (time management), switch gears on the fly (flexibility), and/or build relationships (trust).

Step 2: Now take these examples and create stories with a beginning, middle, and end using the STAR(T) method. Add some personality and take out information that dives too deeply into the details. Each story should be no longer than two minutes. That's why it's important to write them down and practice so you can prevent sidebars or unimportant details from slowing things down. Once you feel comfortable, you'll have five key stories to choose from for any of the obvious questions and the confidence to deliver them.

Strengths and Weaknesses

While this question seems antiquated, some interviewers will still ask about such "areas for development." They may also ask what you are doing to improve them. The goal of this question is to determine if you are self-aware enough to know where you are strong and what you need to work on. But this question can also be a "trap" and used against you if you answer it the wrong way. Claiming you are a perfectionist and never make mistakes is hubris. The weakness should be something you have already overcome or are actively working on. By owning your weakness, you are showing self-awareness and the ability to adapt and change. And everyone has a weakness. The goal is to answer the question directly and with confidence—itself a soft skill.

Most people find it easier to come up with strengths than a "positive sounding" weakness. Some strengths examples include team player, flexible or adaptable to new areas or change, remaining calm in the face of pressure, critical/creative thinker, superior communicator, effective manager or leader who can motivate and empower, problem solver, resourceful, influencer (not the online kind), public speaker, ability to learn quickly. Make sure you have a story in case they ask how you use your strengths at work.

Weaknesses or "areas for development" that don't make you sound like a bad employee are harder to come up with. It can also be challenging to explain a weakness without stumbling. Practicing this answer is just as important as practicing all the others. The key is making sure you explain how you've improved and/or are turning those weaknesses into strengths. Here are some examples of "positive" weaknesses:

→ I tend to raise my hand for exciting new projects even if I don't have the bandwidth, but I've gotten better at letting others have some of those opportunities. (Add two sentences on a project you gave up and what you learned from the other person's accomplishment.)

→ I expect the same commitment, efficiency, and effectiveness of others as I do of myself but that doesn't always happen. As a manager, I have learned that everyone has their own style and process even if they don't match mine. I have worked hard to make sure each person's strengths are enabled and developed to create a versatile team. (Add two sentences on how you helped someone use their strengths to compensate for and improve their weaknesses.)

→ I used to live by the adage "If you want it done right, do it yourself," but I realized I can't do everything. So I have worked hard to empower my team to own their projects, and if they make mistakes or complete it differently than I would, it becomes a great learning and growing experience for them and, at times, for me as well. (Add two sentences on a project where someone took an approach you wouldn't have thought of, and you learned a new way of doing something.)

→ When I started this job, I hadn't been exposed to all the ways that data can be used, and it's been a learning curve. Now I think about data at the start of every project while learning new ways to track results. (Add two sentences about your success using data but also how you now lean on others with specific expertise before starting a new project to make sure you are not missing something.)

→ I'm a critical observer, so when I'm in a large meeting, I tend to listen to everyone else before speaking because I like to hear all the sides and analyze the points being made. Sometimes I don't speak at all if my opinion has been voiced by someone else. I still listen, but now I'm more apt to speak up to make sure my voice is heard when I have an important point to make or information to add to the conversation. (Add two sentences about a recent meeting where when you spoke up and your point was used to catapult a decision or a new way of doing something.)

Notice how the weaknesses really aren't weaknesses, but great qualities to have in an employee. The goal is to add two sentences after each weakness showing your improvement or your own self-awareness of the weakness and steps you are taking to make sure your weakness is not prohibiting your success.

Transitioning Careers

If you make that second interview, the recruiter believes you have transferrable skills and the hiring manager is interested based on the recruiter's feedback. You mission is to keep connecting all the dots. If this is a new career for you, some hard skills may be missing such as using data for decision-making or specific software experience. If you are short on transferrable hard skills, focus on your soft skills; they are always applicable to any job you apply for. Nearly every job requires effective communication skills, strong presentation skills, accountability, decision-making experience, time management skills, and an ability to work in fast-paced or slower-paced environments. The examples you give in the STAR method should highlight those skills that are directly applicable to the job you want.

One of my favorite soft-skill stories I told during interviews was about an A-list singer who wouldn't perform at a major event if she couldn't fly her unmanned drone over the audience and on to the stage to open the show. This represented a huge potential liability, but she was the opening act. The goal was to tell her she couldn't do it but in a way that would still ensure she would show up and perform on opening night. I came up with a solution using FAA **research** and by **leveraging relationships** at the studio. Then I **coached** senior leaders, including the **president** of the cable channel, on what to say to her. We worked it out, she did perform, and it was a win all around. While this was not a situation I would ever have to deal with in HR, it showed I was solution-oriented and could influence leaders with sound advice on how to deal with difficult people in a tense situation. And it was an intriguing story that stands out! You want to be interesting and remembered.

What Questions to Ask

Nearly every interviewer will ask, "Do you have any questions?" And you better have some or you will look like you haven't thought about the job or the company, which will suggest you aren't that interested. Bob Hancock has recruited thousands of people in his career and the one negative he hears over and over from hiring managers is that a candidate had no questions. "It does play in the hiring decision," he said. "Having questions shows you did some research and are curious about the company or the team you would join. Not having any questions gives all hiring managers pause and may lose you the job."

Examples of questions to ask:

→ **To the hiring manager:** What is your management style? How do you keep up on what your reports are doing? What is the one thing the last person in this job could have done better? What happened to the last person in this role? How do you provide feedback to your direct reports? How would you set expectations for the role if I'm fortunate enough to be chosen for this job? Has the culture changed since COVID-19 and, if so, how? What defines success in this role? What one area of the company or within the group do you think could be improved? Why do you like working for [company name]?

→ **To additional interviewers:** Tell me how the company or group has changed during your time here? What one thing would make someone successful in this role? How do you see the person in this role interacting with your function/role? Can you give me a better understanding of the culture here? Has the culture changed since COVID-19 and, if so, how? Would you consider this a fast- or slow-paced environment and can you give me an example? Why do you like working for [company name]? If there is one unwritten rule at this company that everyone eventually figures out, what would that be? What is your best piece of advice for someone onboarding here?

If those don't work for you or you are having trouble coming up with interview questions, check out John Kador's *301 Best Questions to Ask on Your Interview.* **Reminder:** You are allotted a certain amount of time to meet with each interviewer. They likely have another meeting right after yours or another interviewer is waiting at the door. Most interviewers don't want to stay one minute over no matter how much they like you. Therefore, if you are going to ask questions, don't wait until your time is up.

Be careful about asking questions that could be misinterpreted. For example, "How late do people work?" or "Do people work remotely?" or "How much vacation time do people get?" may suggest to them that you are lazy, won't put in the time needed, or are expecting to work from home before proving yourself in the role. Even if having such flexibility or a certain amount of vacation time is part of your values, ask the question in a way that doesn't leave a negative impression. "Tell me about the overall benefits and the company's position on work schedules" is a much more diplomatic approach. Further, hold such questions until later in the recruiting process—don't ask the hiring manager. The recruiter will know the company's culture and have those answers, and since you have already built a relationship with them, they will be less likely to misinterpret the questions.

Prepare Your Psyche

Now that you've established your stories and skills and your thoughts are clear, it's time to prepare your psyche. Walking into an interview should be akin to a football player running on the field to play in a big game: You need the energy and excitement that tells you, "I got this!" To that end, I recommend the following:

1. Quiet time before the interviews. Either take the day off from your current job or arrive at the interview site at least 30 minutes prior, park down the block for 15 minutes, and clear your head of the day's craziness. If it is a video call, take the 30 minutes prior to focus. Meditation is great, but if you aren't into that or fear it will mellow you out too much, simply bring your notes and focus on your stories.

2. Music to pump you up. I'm a big believer of playing a song that energizes you—not the one that gets stuck in your head but the song that makes you want to tap your feet or get your dance on. For me it's "Don't Stop Me Now" (Queen), "Confident" (Demi Lovato), "Just like Fire" (Pink), "Fighter" (Christina Aguilera), or anything Lizzo like "Good as Hell." Get your energy up and your groove on!

3. Power pose. If you're at home prior to the interview or you find a bathroom in the building where the interview will be, bring on that Amy Cuddy "Wonder Woman" stance. That's right: Hands on hips. Legs strong. Head held high. The stance that once again says, "I got this!"

Chapter 14 Summary

1. **Pick five great accomplishments:** Review the job description and list five career accomplishments where you used both hard and soft skills that relate to the job description and the new job.

2. **STAR(T) Method:** Using the STAR(T) (Situation, Task, Action, Result, (Takeaway)) method, create stories around those five accomplishments that incorporate the hard and soft skills needed for the job description and new job.

3. **Strengths and Weaknesses:** Identify your strengths and how you've leveraged them and how you have improved upon or overcome your weaknesses.

4. **Ask questions:** Ask the hiring manager smart questions to show interest in the role.

5. **Psyche yourself up:** Get yourself in the right headspace for the interview. Meditate, say affirmations, play music, do a power pose—whatever works before you start the the interview.

The Hiring Process

"Patience and fortitude conquer all things."

—Ralph Waldo Emerson, American essayist

You may have finished your in-person interviews, but the process isn't over until you start the job. When you are looking for a new job, it is all consuming and top-of-mind *for you*. But the hiring manager is still doing his day job while trying to make the right hire. You are not the hiring manager's sole focus of the day, week, or even month. And a lot happens behind the scenes.

Summary of the Hiring Process

1. A job is posted.

2. The recruiter or hiring manger will search for potential candidates on LinkedIn to "calibrate" the type of experience and profile the hiring manager expects.

3. The recruiter looks through the first 50 profiles of those who applied and, if it is a high-level role, may do additional sourcing on LinkedIn or through private databases.

4. The recruiter either screens a few candidates or presents first-glance candidates to the hiring manager to determine who to pursue.

5. The recruiter completes screening interviews.

6. The recruiter and hiring manager meet or exchange emails to discuss what was learned from the screening interviews.

7. The hiring manager decides if any of the candidates should move to the next round.

8. The recruiter schedules the hiring manager to meet with one or several candidates over the next few days or weeks.

9. The hiring manager does a phone screen with the candidate or, if possible, the candidate is brought on site.

10. The hiring manager and recruiter debrief over which, if any, candidate should move forward in the process.

11. The recruiter schedules the next round of interviews.

12. The hiring manager interviews top candidates on site (if possible) for a second time. Additional interviewers are brought in and/or the candidate is asked to give a presentation.

13. The recruiter, hiring manager, and anyone else who interviewed the candidate debrief on what they learned and whether the candidate has the right skills for the role and will fit within the culture of the company and the team.

14. The hiring manager decides who will move to the next round or if the recruiter should search for new candidates, in which case the process starts over.

15. Candidates who move forward likely come back for a final round of interviews.

16. The hiring manager and interviewers debrief.

17. If a candidate moves toward offer, the hiring manager or recruiter checks references and may seek backdoor references from colleagues.

18. The recruiter works with the hiring manager and compensation leaders to determine an appropriate offer and decide who will present it.

19. The offer is presented verbally to the candidate followed by an offer letter.

20. Negotiation may ensue.

21. Anything outside the standard compensation package for the level and title will need approval from senior leaders including the hiring manager's boss, finance, and HR.

22. Once there's agreement on the compensation package, the candidate is given a small window to sign the offer letter.

23. The candidate signs and a hire is made.

Tip #15: Be patient with the hiring process, which may not fit into your timeline.

The process for each hiring manager is just that—a process—and no two job interview processes will be the same. The goal is to stay in the process without missteps. And an offer is almost always contingent on a background check; that additional paperwork will be sent to the candidate upon acceptance. The entire process can take from two to four months or even longer, so if you made it to the end, congratulate yourself!

Thank-you Notes

Once you finish the in-person interviews, write thank-you notes. Use the opportunity to provide more context about your skills and keep your name top of mind. Back in the '90s and early 2000s, candidates wrote handwritten thank-you notes and sent them via U.S. postal service (aka snail mail). Some people still rely on handwritten thank-you notes, and while noble, the hiring process moves quickly and it may take days for that note to arrive. Further, with more people working from home, interviewers may never receive a thank-you note that is sent to the office. The hiring manager may assume you didn't write one and lean toward another more etiquette savvy candidate. Bob says he's floored at how many candidates don't write thank-you notes: "By not writing a thank-you note, you are sending a message to me and the hiring manager that you are not proactive or not interested in the role."

While that narrative may not be true, forgetting this step could torpedo your candidacy. I once heard a recruiter comment that if a candidate couldn't write a simple note, he or she couldn't be trusted with their business. Fortunately, email is fine. Make sure you at least get one business card if you interviewed in person or you ask the recruiter for the company email address format (e.g., first name.last name@company.com). As a last resort, ask the recruiter to forward your thank-you notes to the respective interviewers for you. Thank-you notes can be simple, but they should also connect the dots between you and the new career and/or cover something that you discussed. Some examples:

> Thank you so much for taking the time to meet with me today. I left even more excited about the role and thinking about how I can add value to the team overall and be a successful collaborator in your complex organization. My in-depth experience in [X] and [Y], combined with my insatiable curiosity to learn, will help me be successful as a [job title] on your dynamic team.
>
> Thank you again and I look forward to hearing from you soon.

or

> Thank you for taking the time to interview me today. I really enjoyed our conversation. It was great to hear your perspective on company culture, accountability, and the incredibly talented people I would be collaborating with should I be fortunate to secure this role. My 20+ years of business experience and ability to learn quickly would allow me to bring a diverse perspective to the role of [title] on your culturally diverse team.
>
> I hope we'll be working together in the near future.

or

> Thank you for taking the time to interview me today. I am excited about the possibility of working with your senior leaders on [A, B, and C]. My 20+ years of business experience, combined with my ability to learn quickly, will allow me to hit the ground running.

If you have any further questions about my background, please don't hesitate to ask. I look forward to hearing from you soon.

What if you bombed one of the interviews? You were asked questions about process and you answered with personal stories. Or you stammered through answers. Put a positive spin on them in the thank-you note:

> Thank you for taking the time to interview me today. While I didn't feel I expressed myself as clearly as I could have on some of your questions, I know I'll be able to bring value to the areas we discussed including [A, B, and/or C] if given the opportunity. My excitement for working at [company name] is even stronger after meeting with your stellar team today.

or

> Thank you for taking the time to interview me today. I am excited about the possibility of working with your senior leaders on [A, B, and C]. My 20+ years of business experience, combined with my ability to learn quickly, will allow me to hit the ground running.
>
> I thought more about the question you asked me about providing an example of a growth mindset. I stumbled in the room but thought of dozens of examples on the way home including [A and B]. As a naturally analytical person, I like to think deeply about questions and provide thorough and thoughtful answers. I hope that helps explain my thought process a little clearer.
>
> If you have any further questions about my background, please don't hesitate to ask. I look forward to hearing from you soon.

These notes address the issue you had but also reinforce the value you would bring to the company. Thank-you notes, like references, may seem like a "formality" but they are part of the hiring process. As a person transitioning careers, leverage your thank-you notes to reiterate the connection between the skills from your old career and those required in your new career while emphasizing your ability to learn quickly.

Projects

I hear often that companies will tell candidates they are finalists and then ask them to execute a project. Some companies provide a specific situation or analysis to assess a candidate's thought process or work product. Too often, candidates provide the work thinking they are shoe-ins for the job, only to never hear from the company again. You just got swindled for free work! And yet how could you say no? In such a case, I suggest you ask if you can instead present a project you completed in the past. If the answer is no, ask if you can present some ideas in verbal form with no leave-behind documentation. If you have done such projects in the past and that work was never acknowledged but you saw some of the results executed on the open market, let them know. It justifies your hesitation.

References

If you haven't received an offer yet but you've been asked for references, there's a good chance you are one of two finalists. Your references may then determine whether you get the job. If you have already received an offer, it could be contingent on your references and a background check.

Every job, whether you love it or hate it, is a place to build relationships with people who could one day sing your praises. A reference will tell a prospective manager at a new company or even the one you work for about your strengths and development areas, your work style, and whether you'd fit in with the culture of the company or team you are trying to join. The best way to ensure your references say something nice about you is to be a top performer with exceptional hard and soft skills. Simple! The more enthusiastic the reference, the better chance you have at securing a dream job.

Step 1: Choosing the Right References

The first step is to find at least three people who are willing to give you a positive reference. Then ask them on the phone or in person if they are comfortable being an enthusiastic reference. Any hesitation means the person is not comfortable even if they don't say so out loud. Never provide a hesitant reference to a prospective employer. Why? Only part of the equation is saying great things about you; the other part is the enthusiasm behind the great things. Enthusiasm is especially important because recruiters and hiring managers will pick up on a tentative or hesitant reference.

I once had a former employee reach out and ask me for a reference. This employee was not a high performer and left my team shortly before being fired. I knew this employee had worked in a few other roles since working for me and there was no way I could give a positive and enthusiastic reference. So I simply said, "I don't think I can give you the enthusiastic reference you need since you haven't worked for me in a few years." Unfortunately, some people think it is easier to just say "Sure" even if they have misgivings, and those references may come back to haunt you.

If everyone you contact is enthusiastic, who do you choose to be a reference? Most recruiters will ask the reference how they know you, so choose managers or colleagues with whom you have closely worked with.

Former/current manager. This person is the ideal reference because former or current managers can tell a prospective employer how you brought value to the team, what projects you worked on, how you built relationships, how you worked cross-functionally, and how you succeeded in the role. However, most job seekers don't want to use a current manager in case the new role at the new company doesn't work out, and that makes sense. Also, if a current manager does give you a reference, some potential employers may wonder if that manager is trying to unload you due to poor performance unless there are special circumstances such as a merger/acquisition, reduction in force, or other issues. But do ask a former manager to be an enthusiastic reference if you left on good terms. If you didn't get along with your former manager, were terminated for performance, or you don't feel he or she would be a positive reference, find someone else in the company.

Current direct reports. I don't recommend asking your direct reports or close team members to be a reference because that reveals you are looking elsewhere. And since you are their boss, the power dynamic could make that direct report very uncomfortable, "forcing" them to say something nice about you when they may not like you or how you manage the team.

Colleagues/co-workers. Former or current colleagues can be exceptional references, especially if they worked directly with you on a complex, cross-functional project. Seek out the highest-titled colleague who is willing to provide you that enthusiastic reference because title means credibility. A co-worker with the same title or at the same level may not be able to view your role from a leadership standpoint, but their support could still make a difference.

Customers/clients. If you work in a customer service–type role and you have a recurring customer, or you work in sales and have clients, consider them as references, especially if they can speak to your ability to solve problems, influence, persuade, and build relationships.

Networking colleagues/college professors. References who haven't actually worked with you are considered character witnesses. They can talk about who you are as a person, such as "Everyone loves [your name]" or "[Your name] is a hard worker." Try to find someone you worked with on a committee or who you negotiated against and can speak to your win-win skills. College students sometimes use professors as references. They can acknowledge that you are a top performer or class leader but can't usually provide insights on real-world experience unless you were a research assistant or worked for them. These references are not as effective as former managers or colleagues who connect the dots from your former career to your new career. Networking colleagues and college professors should be the last option if you can't find more relevant references.

Family and friends. No! Don't use them as a reference even if you worked for a family business. Find someone else in that business or provide a reference from another job. The last thing you want is a recruiter asking, "How do you know the candidate?" and your reference answers, "Oh, he's my cousin!"

Step 2: Preparing References

When I was a manager, I was always shocked when candidates didn't alert their references they were applying for a new role. I would call references and they would ask how the candidate was doing because they hadn't heard from them in a while, or the reference would ask what job the candidate was applying for at what company. It is a lost opportunity if you don't prepare your references to say the right things to help you secure the role. At a minimum, you should make sure they know the following:

a. The job you are interviewing for (provide the job description).

b. Information you were unable or forgot to explain in the interview process that would be helpful to the hiring manager. For example, that you are comfortable working in an ambiguous environment (with an example). Or you are a quick learner (provide an example). Or you are good at digging deep to understand a problem before offering solutions (again, with an example). You may need to remind your reference of your accomplishments and value so they have examples to provide to the recruiter.

c. What skill set is critical for the role and how specific skills you either have or learned in your current career or position transfer directly to the role you are applying to. Provide examples.

d. Qualities that make you a great candidate for the role.

e. Qualities that make you unique out of all the other possible candidates out there. This is where your "unique perspective" on the role comes in and how you have been successful jumping into projects or roles where you knew nothing when you started.

f. Weaknesses or areas for development that you have worked hard to overcome (e.g., you had trouble handing off projects as the company scaled but became successful at quickly adapting to change).

g. If you were terminated from a role for performance and you gave the recruiter or hiring manage an "alternate perspective" to explain your departure, make sure your reference knows that perspective.

h. The importance that their enthusiasm will play in influencing the hiring team.

Discuss the above with all references and/or send bullet points for them to review prior to giving their contact information to a prospective employer.

Step 3. Handling Backdoor References

Some employers no longer ask for references because they know candidates will provide only those who say positive things about them, often with scripted answers. Instead, some employers seek "backdoor" references, meaning someone who has worked with the candidate but isn't on a candidate's reference list. Those types of references can be more genuine in their characterization of a candidate or less genuine if they had a direct conflict with the candidate.

When backdoor references are negative, I tend to dig deeper as a hiring manager and ask, "How long ago did you two work together?" Then I will follow up with, "Does anyone else feel the same way?" I'll ask for specific names and contact information for anyone mentioned. If the reference worked with the candidate more than five years ago and can't provide other people who feel the same way to corroborate their opinion or I'm told the candidate "managed up" well so no one else had a conflict, I am much less willing to rely heavily on their information. Why? People can grow and change from previous experiences. Unfortunately, not everyone is so forgiving.

More than 20 years ago, when I was a TV news reporter, I lost two potential jobs because a former boss gave a negative backdoor reference. How did I know? One recruiter disappeared—commonly known as *ghosting* (more about ghosting on p. 221)—the day after I was told an offer would be coming. None of my references told me the recruiter called them, but the recruiter apparently had called other people I had worked with, including, I presume, my former boss. The other recruiter slipped and admitted, "We got some information and realized you wouldn't be a good fit here." That was my first lesson about relationships and that it doesn't matter if you have great references—negative behavior will linger in the minds of others. It also taught me that my behavior in my 20s was going to haunt me if I didn't do something about it.

I was immature back then but becoming more self-aware and working on myself and my behavior. The bad news was that no one knew I had grown and changed since my first few jobs. I decided to write a letter (no email back then) to that former news director explaining how I had matured, how I would have handled events differently, and how I would hate to be judged in the future for actions in my early 20s. I never heard back, but I also never had a problem securing a job again.

The best way to ensure that everyone you work with has something positive to say about you is to build relationships. Find your champions in every job who know your value. If you notice relationships suffering because you may have offended someone or didn't show your best side, consider a mea culpa even if you believe the other person is wrong. Would you rather be content or contentious? Would you rather be right or employed in your dream job? You can't stop someone from saying something bad about you, but you can grow from every experience and show your growth in the next opportunity.

Silence

If you were asked for references, that is usually the last step before potentially getting an offer. But many companies ask more than one candidate for references. It can take weeks to do reference checks and decide if you are the person the company wants to hire. All that waiting may create a dialogue in your head about what your references are saying or wishing you said something different in the interview stage. I remember saying to my husband days before I received an offer from Roku that I was sad I hadn't heard from the recruiter and I guess I didn't get the job. You may start to question your ability to do the job or convince yourself the company chose someone else. It is amazing what those six inches between your ears can do to your confidence! If you are waiting in silence, it usually means one of two things:

1. You're #2. The company made an offer to the top-choice candidate first. That may feel like failure but it's not. As a person transitioning careers, making it to #2 is a win! That means it's just a matter of time before you become a hiring manager's top candidate. It's also important to recognize that some companies can't see outside the box and won't hire someone without the exact skills. Square pegs, square holes. Those companies dream of being progressive, but in the end, they fall back on the safe choice. Sometimes the top candidate skills are no different from yours, but they have worked in the same industry and you haven't. Both of those happened to me when I was interviewing at Intuitive.

I interviewed for an HR Business Partner role to support the chief medical officer. I now had more than two years of traditional HR Business Partner experience plus 20 years of business experience. The recruiter told me I was a finalist for the role with two other people. Then it was down to me and one other person. The person hired had supported a chief medical officer in a previous role in a med-tech company. I could boast neither of those. Not only that, the hiring manager was also moving into a new role supporting the chief medical officer and other senior leaders. While strategic HR business partnering is similar in most tech companies, I understood why the other candidate was hired; his experience would allow him to ramp the hiring manager quicker on how that side of the business works.

I expressed my disappointment and asked to be considered for future opportunities. That was my way of asking for feedback or determine if my candidacy was over at that company for good. I had made it to the end and wanted to hear what I could have done better or what I could learn from the experience. "You belong here," the executive recruiter said. "We just had someone who had experience supporting a chief medical officer. But one of the people you interviewed with is about to have an opening and she'd like to continue the conversation with you." That may sound like a "line," but a few weeks later, the new hiring manager called me, we grabbed coffee, and she hired me a few months later. And the person they hired for the first role? I met him my first day of work in the cafeteria and immediately realized why he was hired for the previous role. It wasn't just his experience, but his calm demeanor. My bubbly personality worked better with a sales organization. That's why you need to stay positive and use every interview experience to hone your message so when a hiring manager is ready to take a risk, you are ready.

2. Ghosting. Unfortunately, the other reason why you may not have heard back from a company is called *ghosting*. I don't condone this rude behavior, but it can happen at any point in the process once the recruiting process has started. While it would be nice to have closure, if a company loses interest at any point in the process, you may never hear another word. What did you do wrong? Maybe your initial screen or the panel interviews didn't go as well as you thought, your references weren't as enthusiastic as the other finalists', or the company got an unflattering backdoor reference. Sometimes headcount gets reallocated to another role, the job description changed based on business needs, or the company decided to hire internally. Sometimes two external recruiters are working to fill the same position and the one you're not talking to found the perfect candidate. There are lots of reasons that could have nothing to do with you—and you may never know why.

How do you find out if you've been ghosted and the process didn't stall due to the hiring manager's unexpected illness? Check in via email or phone call. It's painless. Just don't have expectations. If a company is really interested in a candidate, it will normally keep the candidate "warm," meaning the recruiter or hiring manager will stay in contact with updates. After two emails or voicemail follow-ups, it is time to let go. A company that doesn't even give you a courtesy call or email to let you know you are no longer being considered isn't a company you will want to work for anyway. Time to play Taylor Swift's "Shake It Off" and move on.

On the flip side, the ancient proverb "Two wrongs don't make a right" comes to mind. If you've been ghosted in the past, that's no reason to ghost a potential employer during the interview process or after you have an offer! Once you have engaged in the interview process and taken the recruiter screen, you have an obligation to let the recruiter know if you want to be removed from the process. Disappearing leaves a bad impression and can make the recruiter look bad, especially if you have already been pitched as a candidate to the hiring manager.

I remember a candidate who filled out all their pre-employment paperwork and was scheduled to arrive at headquarters his first day but never showed up. No call. No email. I watched the recruiter try in vain to reach the candidate via phone and email with no response. After a day of attempts, the recruiter asked the local police to do a welfare check. One knock on their door confirmed the candidate was fine. He then wrote a nasty email to the recruiter saying he had changed his mind about the role, that the recruiter went too far sending the police to his house, and to "chill out." WHAT?! Yes, that recruiter's caring about someone's well-being apparently went "too far." It takes a simple phone call to say you are no longer interested, changed your mind, have another offer, or that something else came up. Much better than the police showing up at your house! And remember: Recruiters move! Hiring managers move! And they both have long memories.

You Get an Offer

Not all hiring processes end in rejection. Sometimes you get an offer! You have four ways to respond:

1. Accept immediately.
2. Say you want to review it with a significant other.
3. Say you want to think about it and will respond on a specific day.
4. If the salary isn't what you want, say that it came in a bit lower than you were hoping for.

Taking a day or two to contemplate an offer will not result in it being rescinded. Making a job move is a big deal. Are there any outstanding questions about the compensation package and benefits? Do you understand how much paid time off you will have? Do you know how long the commute is and does that matter? Will you be expected to be in the office or mostly work from home? Just because you made it to the finish line doesn't mean you are done. Rethink how every aspect of your life will change and then decide if you want to change jobs. And if the salary isn't where you want/need it to be, it's time to negotiate.

Negotiating

I could write an entire book about negotiating, but some masterful writers have already done that. I highly recommend *Ask for It*[1] by Linda Babcock and Sara Laschever and *Getting to Yes*[2] by Roger Fisher, William Ury, and Bruce Patton. Both destigmatize what for many is a scary notion, stating it doesn't have to be uncomfortable, contentious, or adversarial. Negotiating your salary for a new job should be as simple as negotiating with your kids ("If you finish your homework, then you can watch TV tonight.") or with your spouse ("It's important for me to eat healthy this week because I have to fit into my dress for an event this weekend, so can we eat at a Mediterranean restaurant tonight and a Mexican restaurant after the event?"). *Ask for It* says to view negotiating as a tool to help bring about change when the desired result is dependent on the cooperation of others. Look at salary negotiations as creating a mutually beneficial agreement where everyone agrees about your value within the parameters of the role and budget.

First, review the amount of cash you need to support yourself and your family. If you didn't do this in Chapter 13, now is the time. Make adjustments based on how your lifestyle may have changed. Once you've come up with a monthly number and are clear on the value you will bring to the role, you are ready to determine what each side's interests are. Let's start with you.

What is most important to you and in what order: salary, bonus, equity, benefits, 401K match, cash incentives (i.e., recognition/spot bonuses)? If you want to transition careers, are you willing to sacrifice financially to do it? Or did you go back to school and want a higher salary to pay off a student loan? Is a certain title important to you to show you are moving forward in your career or are you willing to take a step backward in title for a longer-term gain?

When I transitioned from a legal role in production risk to HR Business Partner, I went from VP to director. I also went from managing a team to an independent contributor. In my mind, I wanted to make sure I understood the new career and role before managing a team again. At the time, I didn't realize how much I'd miss managing, and I plan to get back to that in the near future. But while transitioning into the new role, it wasn't important. Title is aligned with compensation, and as long as the money didn't go down too much, I was fine. Assuming the new job meets all or most of your values, knowing your compensation needs before interviewing for jobs is an important step as you plan your transition to a new career. It will also help you understand how your interests align with the offer and the company's interests.

Once you understand your own interests, ask questions about the entire compensation package to learn if your needs are aligned, but don't let those needs make you inflexible to options if they don't line up exactly. For example, you need $100,000 per year to survive but the company is offering you $80,000 plus a 25% bonus. It is not exactly what you wanted, but with the bonus, the compensation brings you to $100,000. If you're wondering how you'll survive on the $80,000 until the hoped-for bonus, you have two options: (1) Ask for more salary, but it will be hard to bump the offer a full $20,000, or (2) Ask the company for a $20,000+ signing bonus to bridge the gap until you receive that bonus the first year. Signing bonuses are usually reserved for higher-level positions but it never hurts to ask, especially if you explain how such a bonus would make you "whole." Note that signing bonuses are taxed at the highest rate and it's a one-time payment, so it is always better to get even a few thousand dollars more in your salary, which will also mean more money in your bonus if it's a percentage of your base pay.

It is also important to understand how equity plays into a compensation package. Equity is a complicated subject and during my time in HR, I learned that most people early in their careers don't understand the difference between Restricted Stock Units (RSUs) and stock options, vesting schedules, when taxes need to be paid, and how equity can enhance your overall compensation package. I was like that, too, even when I became a VP at Viacom. I received an annual RSU grant and put the letter explaining the grant into a desk drawer. When I started working for a pre-IPO company (Roku) and was granted pre-IPO options, I educated myself about equity. Don't be afraid to ask questions about the equity being offered, and then research the value of that equity and how it may or may not enhance your overall compensation package.

My broker and investment advisor has told me horror stories about people who worked hard their whole lives and never understood investing. I am still not great at it but I'm learning. If you want to know more about investing, try *The Wall Street Journal: Complete Money and Investing Guidebook* by Dave Kansas.[3] It lays out a detailed explanation of the history of the stock market, Wall Street, investing, and the basics about different types of equity like mutual funds, bonds, and stock. If you want something more conversational so you understand how to invest and save for retirement, I recommend *More than a Millionaire* by Randy Thurman,[4] CEO of Retirement Investment Advisors and a certified financial planner who works with high net-worth individuals. His book is a comprehensive blend of investing fundamentals and strategies for increasing income while living a fulfilling life.

Once you identify your interests, *Ask for It* suggests determining if they could be perceived in a negative light and ruin your opportunity to negotiate a great deal or result in the company pulling back the offer. For example, did you tell the recruiter about an upcoming two-week family vacation and that you would like to start the new job after you come back? Or you want the company to cover the vacation with full pay even though you haven't accrued vacation time yet? Did you already tell the recruiter that you are fine with the salary range presented earlier in the process but now you want a figure outside that range? Did a sudden life event, such as a significant other being laid off, change the amount of money you need to survive? If you are going to spring any surprises in your upcoming negotiation, plan your strategy for them.

In talking to recruiters, here are their top six pet peeves when negotiating with a prospective candidate, any of which could cause the company to rescind their offer:

1. Candidates who try to negotiate every point in the compensation package. Don't create a list of changes you "must have" in the compensation package. This will leave the impression that you are demanding and unable to prioritize. It will also suggest that you are ungrateful for the offer as presented if you want to change every aspect of it. Pick one or two of the most important components to discuss and negotiate.

2. Candidates who want a package that matches their current employment. Every company handles compensation differently. Some put more emphasis on cash salary while others give a hefty bonus at the end of the year. Some companies include equity as part of "Total Rewards" and look at the offer holistically with the value of equity included. Others consider equity as "icing on the cake." Alissa from The Winford Group told me about a candidate who absolutely needed her gym membership covered because her current employer did so. She didn't care that she'd be paid more at the new job and could afford the membership on her own or that she would have equity for the first time to enhance her overall compensation. The candidate wouldn't budge, and the company rescinded its offer. The candidate also lost the recruiter's support to submit her for future job opportunities.

3. Candidates who send lengthy emails reiterating previous discussion points and providing detailed analysis of why candidate is correct. Once you have asked for a few adjustments in the package, don't send lengthy emails with a detailed analysis defending your requests. If you are negotiating via email, be concise without too much detail. If you appear too greedy or uninformed, it could look like your priorities are in the wrong place.

4. Candidates who do not express enough interest in the role. You need to re-express your interest in the role at the beginning and end of each conversation and in every thank-you note and email or you may appear to be more interested in the money than the position and the company. Bob Hancock says that when a candidate is only focused on what he/she wants, it feels as if they are using the company to pressure their current employer for a counter-offer and don't actually want the offered role.

5. Candidates who become combative. Some candidates treat a negotiation like a contest between them and the company. Don't do this! These are the people you are going to be working with! Just because you are a lawyer hired to negotiate big contracts doesn't mean you have to "win" in negotiating compensation. If you become adversarial, you will lose the job because you are giving the impression that you don't know how to effectively influence. I have heard of offers being pulled because of such negative vibes during negotiations.

6. Candidates who don't ask for something and then have a chip on their shoulder when they start the job. If you don't ask—and ask appropriately—you won't get what you want. That said, if you do ask and don't get what you want, decide if it's a deal-breaker. If you still accept the job, you can't walk in disgruntled because of what you didn't get. I remember in a first meeting with an employee how he told me he was offered so much more from Facebook and Google and that he was underpaid in his new role, which started a mere four weeks earlier. It definitely left a negative impression on me. You need to move forward with the best positive attitude and be committed to the role after you accept the job. Don't talk about how much of a paycut you took or other offers you turned down or how much you "sacrificed" to get there.

How you handle negotiations will set the tone for how you enter the company. Nuff said!

Now you're ready to negotiate based on *your* interests but you still need to outline the company's interests. The best way to do that is to listen closely to what is being said during the interview process and in the offer being made and then ask questions. The company wants to hire you—that is the good news. But the hiring manager can only hire you within the confines of the company's compensation philosophy. Most companies have an interest in being perceived as paying employees fairly, attracting and retaining talented people, and motivating employees to help the company succeed while also supporting the company's overall business strategy. That means the company has a "total rewards" strategy that encompasses compensation, benefits, and short- and long-term incentive programs (like a 401K retirement program with an employer match, a sabbatical after so many years of work, and so on).

Discovering Company Compensation Philosophy

For most jobs, companies may offer cash, quarterly and/or annual bonuses, and/or equity as part of total cash compensation; and/or, in some circumstances, instant cash rewards such as spot bonuses. Some companies pay all cash while others offer a combination of other incentives. By understanding some basics about the company's interests, you will be a better negotiator. Here are a few questions to ask about the company's compensation philosophy:

1. Does the company's compensation philosophy lead, match, or lag the market? Companies will always end up in one of three compensation positions: leading, matching, or lagging the market. To answer this question, you first need to know how companies view "the market." For most, the "market" is determined from data that comes from employment survey companies such as Radford, Croner, and iMercer. They provide broad job data across multiple industries (e.g., data science jobs in all industries) or narrow data in a specific industry and size of company (e.g., all data science jobs in technology companies with fewer than 10,000 people). Depending on what information a company pays for and what companies are in the survey, salary ranges could be on target or very wrong. Also, companies don't always use the most recent surveys, so they are not always credible or keep up with the current economy. In a hot job market, salaries tend to rise because of competition, so candidates may have expectations that are much higher than the data. Also, survey data can be more regionally focused or city focused. An average job salary in the state of New York will most likely be different than what it is in New York City.

Most companies will look at market data in the city where a candidate will be working. A person who works in public relations in San Francisco will likely be paid more than a similar position in Oklahoma City. Some jobs, such as software engineer and data scientist roles, are so "hot" that they may be compensated similarly no matter where they are located. Companies have a ton of data on the market and what people should be paid for certain jobs. You can also find a lot of data online through Salary.com, Payscale.com, Monster.com, and Glassdoor. Knowing this data, you can ask smart questions to find out if a company is trying to hire you cheaply or its offer is low because the company's philosophy is to lag the market.

When I moved to Viacom, I was offered a higher title and, therefore, a higher salary than when I was at NBC. That said, I didn't ask the right questions and had no idea Viacom at the time was well known as lagging the market in salary and benefits compared to its competitors like Discovery and AMC and the major networks. A company may choose to lag the market because its culture is strong enough to attract and retain great talent, and this was true with Viacom, which for years was led by the immensely popular MTV and Nickelodeon. And since I was being offered a higher title and more money, I didn't even think to negotiate or check the market.

Roku, on the other hand, paid market rate in compensation and benefits for employees and new hires, which means it matched at least the 50th percentile of the range for a particular role. For example, if total compensation (cash, bonus) ranged from $50,000 for a less-experienced person to $100,000 for the most experienced, the offer may come in around $75,000.

Some companies like Netflix are well known to lead the market or pay higher salaries and/or benefits to attract and retain the best employees. That doesn't mean they'll always pay top of the market; it means the company will pay more than 75% and sometimes over 100% of the market for the right candidate. But there can be a price to pay. At Netflix, it is well known that vacations are fine as long as you aren't stalling business. It is not uncommon to answer emails and calls at night, on weekends, and even on vacation. That's why you need to know what is most important to you because if culture, personal time, or something other than compensation is a priority and you understand a company's compensation philosophy, you will know if the offer is fair and will work for your lifestyle.

2. How are bonuses calculated? Incentive pay or "bonuses" may be offered by some companies to both motivate and compensate high performance in driving business results. Each company tailors their incentive pay program to fit the company's goals, and which can also be used to differentiate employees based on performance. You may be offered more cash and less incentive pay at one company and the exact opposite at another. Ask questions to understand how much of the bonus calculation is based on your performance versus the company's performance. You will also need to know what percentage of your overall pay the bonus will be based on. If your bonus is based on a percentage of your salary, you will want start with the highest salary possible.

3. Are there any other cash incentives such as spot bonuses or a 401K match? Some companies reward individuals for great work with spot bonuses. Managers and sometimes employees can send company-financed cash rewards to colleagues for their performance on certain projects, and employees can use those cash rewards for whatever they want. It is quite incentivizing and makes employees feel good when someone recognizes their hard work. But you can't control if or when you receive one. Better to focus on guaranteed money such as a 401K match where you control how much you put in, up to maximizing the match if the company offers one. These matches can seem like modest amounts, but it is free money and it adds up! Find out if your prospective employer offers such a 401K match as part of the overall package.

4. How do employees receive raises and promotions? The most common compensation system is "pay for performance" based on yearly evaluations and/or yearly base-pay increases. Two people performing the same job title may not be compensated the same amount because one is working at a higher level and outperforming the other. There is also market compensation where an employee is paid within the market range for the role based on their years of experience—although the employee won't see an increase until the market ranges change, their role expands, or they get promoted. Learn how to "move your pay up" before you start at the new company but be careful how you ask about it. If you focus too soon on how to get promoted, it may seem as if you don't want the job or the salary being offered or won't focus on the job you are being offered. You will want to ask this question generically; for example, "What would be considered 'exceeding expectations' in this role or working at a higher level?" or "Tell me about your annual review process and how merit increases are allocated?" These questions are better for the recruiter than the hiring manager. The recruiter is at the finish line of filling the role, and if you ask appropriately, the recruiter may not tell the hiring manager, who might misinterpret your intent.

5. What is the company's equity philosophy? Knowing who or what levels of the organization receives equity will keep you from asking for something the company can't provide. Start by asking a simple question such as "Is there equity?" or "Who receives equity at the company?" If there is equity, follow up with, "Are there annual grants and how are those decided?" Every company that offers equity has an equity plan. They are long and comprehensive; few companies will provide a copy, so you most likely will need to negotiate without seeing it. If the company is pre-IPO (not public yet), it is good to know what happens to your equity if the company is sold or if the company goes public.

Knowing all aspects of the company's compensation and equity philosophies will help you understand what is behind the company's offer and whether you have wiggle room to ask for more.

Chapter 15 Summary

1. **Thank-you notes.** Use these notes to connect your experience and skills with the new role and remind potential employers of what you would bring.

2. **References.** Prepare your references to help them further the message of how your experiences (with examples) have prepared you for the new career.

3. **Review your interests.** Review what is most important to you in the negotiation such as cash, bonus, equity, and title to be clear on which to focus on.

4. **Know the company's interests.** Gain as much knowledge as you can about the company, compensation, equity plans, and your role's market value to understand the company's interests.

16

A Classy Exit

"Don't cry because it's over. Smile because it happened."
—Dr. Seuss, children's author

You got the job! You accepted the offer! Now what? Breathe. Smile. And know the journey ahead of you is exciting. If you had a great boss, express your gratefulness. If you had a bad experience, be gracious in your departure because your current role has led you to this new career or job. No matter which experience you had, the exit path is the same, and it starts with giving your boss at least two weeks' notice. Yes, notice. You don't get to quit instantly, tell him or her off, or delete every file you've ever worked on. It doesn't matter how much of a jerk your boss is, how much the company "screwed you," or how much you want your boss to know how you feel. Simply tell your boss you have another offer that you have accepted and your last day will be two weeks from the day you have this conversation. This is an in-person conversation even if in person is on Zoom. I have known people to email their bosses if their boss is traveling or there is

Tip #16: Leave a company with dignity and show respect for your time there.

so much bad blood that a conversation would lead to more personal trauma. That is understandable, but never stay in a job like that again!

I get it. I had one boss who never contacted me after I gave notice—not even on my last day. I had to leave her a voicemail. Then she tried to Facebook friend me a week after I was gone. Not kidding! I wanted to give another boss a piece of my mind and didn't, but wish I had. Another boss lied to me when trying to get me to stay after pressure from other senior leaders. Once I called my boss's boss to explain why I was leaving. What did it accomplish? Nothing, except make me look like a complainer. That boss is still employed in the same job and I regretted that conversation immediately after.

When I planned to leave Roku, I was in the middle of helping a leader with change management on a huge reorg and knew I had to finish it. I had been working on it for months and it would culminate in about three weeks. Could I have put in two weeks' notice? Yes, but that would have left all those people affected by the reorg in the hands of my boss who wasn't involved in the change management plan. That wouldn't have been fair to my boss or the leader who had to manage through the change or the employees affected. So I stayed for three weeks, worked my butt off, and kept my departure quiet. Most people found out I was leaving during my last few days at the company and I left with my dignity intact—it was the right thing to do. The leader said to me, "How you leave a company says a lot about who you are." He was right. I believed in helping people and I wasn't going to leave that in someone else's hands.

Your attitude should look forward, not back. Don't burn bridges. You never know if your paths will cross again. Here's how to leave a company with class:

Preparing Your Company and Team for Your Departure

1. Written notice. Once you tell your boss you are departing, he/she will usually ask for something in writing with an end date. And I will say it again: You must give two weeks' notice. No matter how much you may hate your role, don't leave in a huff and quit without proper notice. Your written communication should not include grievances. It should be positive and upbeat, thanking your boss for the opportunity to work at the company. For example:

Hi [boss's name],

As we discussed on the phone, this is my official notice of departure, with my last day being [date]. I have truly enjoyed my time here and my ability to contribute to such a stellar team/company. I wish the company nothing but the best and hope our professional paths cross again in the future.

Thank you,

[your name]

Even if you have issues with your boss or the company, write a professional note:

Hi [boss's name],

Please accept this email as my formal resignation. My last day will be [date]. I wish you the best of luck in the future.

Thanks,

[your name]

You should also send a goodbye email to vendors, external clients, and contacts. It should be simple and provide information about who to contact in your absence. For example:

Dear [name of contact]:

It has been a pleasure working with you for the past [number of] years. I have made the choice to depart [name of company]. Please contact [name of colleague/new contact] in the future. [His/Her/Their] contact information is below. I wish you all the best and hope our professional paths cross in the future.

[Add contact information for new contact.]

Best,

[your name]

Before you put in your notice, make a list of the people you want to say goodbye to in case you need to send them an email from your personal account. If you put in your notice and get kicked out that day, which will most likely happen if you go to a competitor, accept it and move on. Keep it professional even though you are no longer with the company.

2. Transition your work. Your goal is to leave the company, team, and co-workers with all the information they need to carry on your responsibilities including a roadmap for where to find files. You may be leaving, but life continues for those you leave behind. Build a list of where files are stored and pass on historical and current information as quickly as possible to prevent deadlines from being missed or cross-functional partners from being negatively affected. Also, forward important emails to those who may need them. It's your job to make sure that business can seamlessly continue without you.

3. Train up your team. If you are a manager, it is your job to train up your team on all the things you may have shielded them from. Make sure they know how to deal with office politics, how to handle controversial matters, and how to be self-sufficient without your leadership. Your success in training them will depend on the maturity of your team, of course, but you need to do everything you can to make sure they are taken care of and have the knowledge they need to carry on with their jobs.

4. Don't badmouth or gossip. Your job is to leave on a high note. You are the one leaving, so if you badmouth the company, you are badmouthing your colleagues' workplace. And while you may hate your boss, you will be seen as a "problem person" if you dump your grievances. If HR asks for an exit interview, leave out your emotion and opinions; just state the facts about how your boss or team or company may be failing in a constructive, actionable way. Any complaining will be dismissed as the gripes of a disgruntled—and—departing employee.

5. Don't say anything you can't back up with facts. Unfortunately, I have been privy to numerous terminations and voluntary departures.

In exit interviews, I have often heard "hostile work environment" or "harassment" or "discrimination." If those are true, you should have brought them to HR's attention much earlier than on your way out the door. If you feared retaliation or not being heard and waited for your exit interview to bring them up, be willing to discuss the experiences that led to that level of accusation. Speak your heart with dates, times, and facts. HR is obligated to investigate, and you may be saving your colleagues from the same.

6. Social Media. If you left with class, don't ruin it on social media with a lengthy missive about how much you hated your old job, boss, colleagues, or company. As Frank Sinatra once said, "The best revenge is massive success." Go out and get it.

7. Draft an uplifting goodbye note. Your parting note should talk about how far the company/projects have come and how much enthusiasm you have for the company's future. Don't mention your new employer if writing from your work email but do include personal contact information. LinkedIn will inform everyone where you moved to if your settings allow, so focus on the past and present about the company you are leaving and not the future.

Take Time to Relax and Reflect

With that you have departed. Now what? I hope you have taken at least a few days off before starting your new job. No matter how great the experience at your last job, being able to decompress between jobs is critical to the success in your new role. It is even more critical if you are leaving a bad situation because you may experience PTSD-like symptoms in trying to move forward. Take the time to breathe, take walks, and reflect. Look back at all the things that went right in your last job and if there is anything you would change. Then think about how you want to enter the new job. If you are starting a new career *and* a new job, then believe in your reinvention and own the new you.

Chapter 16 Summary

1. **Resign.** Resign in person—or in this work-from-home era, via video call or at least verbally—to your boss and then in written form so your exit can be processed.

2. **Transition work.** Create a roadmap of where to find key files and transfer emails to those who will be handling your work upon your departure.

3. **Train up your team.** Departing managers should help the interim manager or the team understand what they normally would not have visibility to.

4. **Leave classy.** Leave with respect. Don't gossip, complain on social media, or create drama in your departure. Send a goodbye note that thanks the company for your time there.

5. **Take time to relax.** Take time before you start the next job to reflect upon your previous role and company, the good and bad. Determine how you want to enter the new job and what you may do differently.

CHAPTER

17

The First 90 Days

"Starting a new job is always scary, or at least to me it's always scary. It's like the first day of school."

—Sean Maher, actor

Landing a new job in your new career is just the beginning. The hiring manager believed in your capacity to learn and transfer your skills; now you need to do just that. At the same time, if you entered the position at a reasonably high level due to your accumulated years of experience, you will need to quickly build credibility. Recall what I wrote in Chapter 5: The problem with trying to truly understand the (new) career is . . . you can't . . . . "Since you haven't lived it yet, you will need to learn as much as you can about it and speak in ways that show you've done your homework and are serious about moving into that career." That preparation worked for the interview process, but now that you have arrived, the real work of learning and performing begins.

Tip #17: Keep an open mind while confidently learning about the role.

Imposter syndrome describes a condition when people feel like they are pretending to be someone they are not. If you believe you are an imposter, you won't be open to learning quickly because you will be too busy trying to prove what you *do* know so others won't discover you're an "imposter." But that strategy will likely backfire, making you appear arrogant or misinformed. You will lose an opportunity to learn the job from those who have been doing it for years. The reality is that you are *not* an imposter. You are bringing unique skills and a unique perspective to the job. You just need to learn the nuances.

When I started my first HR job at Roku, I had never fired someone, never dealt with a compensation review, never orchestrated an org design or "reorg" with a comprehensive change management plan, and never formally coached internally. I had never worked in HR! Those six inches between my ears got the best of me as I worried whether I'd be "found out" because I was entering the company as a director in HR, a higher level than others who had been in HR for years. However, that lack of confidence helped me to be vulnerable enough to know the value of listening, asking questions, learning expectations, and building relationships.

Listen

When starting any new job, whether it is in the same or a new field, the same or a new industry, the most important thing to do is listen. Co-Active Coaching trains coaches to understand there are three levels of listening.[1] Level One is when you are listening from inside your own head. While someone is talking, you are thinking about when you can interject your thoughts or that you forgot to defrost dinner or that you wish you had had a better night's sleep. Level One listening means you are only half listening—not really listening at all. In Level Two listening, "you are intensely focused on what the other person is saying. Nothing's distracting you. Thoughts about the past or the future don't intrude." You are fully with the person, hearing what they are saying so that your own thoughts don't enter your mind. Level Three listening is Level Two plus: "You hear more than just the words they're saying. You pick up on all sorts of other things—body language, the inflections and tone of their voice, their pauses and hesitations." You are listening from a more expansive perspective. Most of us are Level One or Level Two listeners. When listening on a new job, you want to be in Level Three as often as possible. From there it is easier to discern if someone is telling you the truth or holding back. You will pick up on whether someone is comfortable or uncomfortable talking to you.

If you are fortunate to receive feedback from your boss or colleagues within the first 90 days, listen closely to understand what it means as far as adjusting your work style to the culture. When I was scheduling introductions with stakeholders at Roku, I was super excited. I had secured my first HR job and was putting time on people's calendars to meet and say hello. Little did I know that two of the teams had been dealing with a major internal matter.

During one of those meet and greets, an employee in the legal department sat in front of me with her arms crossed while I was smiling, warm, and inviting, explaining that I was just trying to get to know key people. "Uh-huh," she said. I told her I was excited to be at Roku and looking to learn and understand the business and culture and would love any insight she could share. "Okay," she said. I then asked if she had been here long. "Yes." I kept trying to be light-hearted, but after ten minutes of one-word answers, I started talking about my family, San Jose, the weather—anything to fill up our time. When I met with two other people in legal and one in marketing, I had a similarly icy greeting, but was able to break through within the first ten minutes. Still, I knew something was up but couldn't figure out what.

The next day as I was walking past my boss's office, he said, "Hey, take it down a notch. You're scaring people." I was like, What!? I was happy, friendly, chatty. I was listening to people describe what was and wasn't working. How could I be scaring them? I went home that night concerned and thought about it overnight. Then it hit me: I was sending those invites as a director in HR! And in the meetings, I was filling dead air with small talk in my overly exuberant way. Most people only know HR as the place to go if you have a problem or are in trouble! And here I was, yapping away, and expecting people to open up to me as if I was just another colleague. From that day forward, I just walked the floor from cube to cube to say hello, and if someone wanted some time, I offered to meet with them right then or suggested putting time on my calendar. I also stopped filling the silence. When I stopped talking, others started!

While my boss's feedback wasn't exactly clear, I figured out what was wrong and how to adjust. Listening to feedback will help you course-correct quickly. And that employee who had her arms crossed? She found me in the cafeteria a few days later, apologized, and wanted to redo our meeting. Sure enough, she thought I was there to fire people. Years later, we laughed about it when she and another lawyer took me out for a farewell lunch before I left the company.

Ask Questions

Now that you know how to truly listen, ask smart questions. Enter the new company as a blank slate so you can learn. Forget the preconceived assumptions you had of your position and the company from your research and interviews. Now is the time to be curious about every aspect of both your job and the business. I knew nothing about traditional HR when I entered Roku, but since I entered as a director and didn't want to be perceived as junior, I asked, "How do you terminate people HERE?" and "How do you view compensation HERE?" I remember asking one co-worker about the company's termination policy and her description felt cold and uncaring, which didn't feel authentic to me. When I asked my boss how *he* conducted terminations, I got a completely different answer, which was more about leaving the employee in the best way possible under the circumstances. This felt more authentic to who I wanted to be in such a difficult moment. Lesson learned: It is always good to ask more than one person how they handle sensitive issues.

In essence, what you do in those first 90 days is learn about the business before trying to make an impact. Ask questions about the company's products, how it generates revenue, how your work impacts the business, how the culture influences the business. Ask questions that help you understand the broader context of your work. As you learn about the business, you will undoubtedly learn about "problems." Every company has something held together by a paperclip and a Band-Aid which may have been working just fine for a long time. If you come in with an immediate solution of a binder clip without learning how and why the company addressed the problem as it did, you risk insulting every person who has been holding it together with the paperclip and Band-Aid.

Therefore, seek to understand the history of the problem first, how the paperclip and Band-Aid came to be, and whether they are still working. If they are, then tuck that binder clip away until it is needed. If they aren't, ask if anyone thought to use a binder clip. If someone tried that idea and failed, then you look like a curious person trying to learn the business. If no one had thought of it, you may turn out to be a hero. Either way, the right questions show that you respect the history and the people who brought the company to this point and are willing to collaborate on a solution without looking like a "savior."

Ultimately, understanding the business will allow you to be more effective, more quickly, and help you to be more strategic in your approach to influencing big decisions. Learning about the business never ends. No matter what level you are, stay apprised of trends, products, and competitors. Keep powerful questions in your toolkit to use when you need them. If you truly listen to the answers, each question will take you closer to the knowledge needed for success.

Understand the Expectations of the Role

My boss at Roku explained his expectations clearly: In the first 30 days, he wanted me to just listen and learn about the business. After 60 days, he expected me to be doing most of the job. In 90 days, he expected me to be fully performing my job. So I took meet and greets in the first 30 days, asked questions, and listened. Sixty days later I was fully invested in all the problems in the departments I supported and had a lot of "firsts": first termination, first compensation review, first leave of absence, first investigation, first HR data analysis. By the time I hit 90 days, it felt like I had been in the role for years. I was coaching leaders to resolve problems and my stakeholders were happy.

When I first started as an HR Business Partner, I never asked about expectations. And having no prior experience in such a role, I tried to be everything to everybody. As an innate people pleaser, I thought being involved in the most minutiae of problems while tackling the bigger org designs and leadership development matters was bringing value to the organization. It was, but it was killing me. By the time I left Roku, I was working nights, weekends, and early mornings long before the sun came up. I thrived on the fast pace and feeling "needed," but the treadmill was wearing me down.

When I moved to Intuitive, I had a completely different experience. Now I had more than two years of HR Business Partner experience and knew the role. I was more confident in knowing what to expect, but I still didn't ask the most important questions to align the expectations of my stakeholders with my expectations of the role. That lack of understanding could have ruined an amazing opportunity. Since I thought I knew the role, I performed it the same way I did at Roku: trying to get an "early win." While taking meet and greets, listening intently, and offering what I felt was sage advice when asked, I noticed the reception was cool. I didn't realize that the way to bring value at Intuitive would be vastly different than how I brought value at Roku despite the same title.

We all bring experiences from other jobs to new roles. Even though I had two years of HR experience, I needed to enter this role with a blank slate and learn not just about the business but also how this role worked in this company. I went from working in a 1,200-person company at Roku to one with 5,000+ people. I also went from entertainment, which is loosely regulated, to the highly regulated med-tech industry. And finally, I went from a "sports team" culture with little employee engagement to a company that treated its employees like family. One wasn't better than the other; they were simply different. And while the differences between companies may seem obvious, it is not always as obvious that the role you are doing will be different as well. That's why asking your stakeholders and your boss how they perceive your role is critical to success. Aligning with your stakeholders' expectations will inform you how to bring value to each stakeholder individually and ultimately the company.

Build Relationships

No matter what role you transition into, you will need to build relationships. Relationships aren't about having commonalities or laughing together. They are built from trust and can't be rushed. If you want a comprehensive guide on how to build trust, I recommend *Trust & Betrayal in the Workplace: Building Effective Relationships in Your Organization* by Dr. Dennis and Dr. Michelle Reina.[2] The Reinas go into detail on the three dimensions of building trust including Trust of Capability, Trust of Character, and Trust of Communication. This model equips people and teams with a shared understanding of how trust is built, how it's broken, and how it's rebuilt.

During the first 90 days of any job, you are a "newbie" and newbies get some slack for not knowing the answer to every question or how to solve every problem. But every interaction, just like an interview, is your first impression. I have heard people immediately state after meeting a new leader, "I don't know about [X]." When probed further, the employee will state that the leader talked the whole conversation, or didn't listen or ask any questions, or already said how to do something better without understanding the business. Breaking trust early in your new job, without even realizing it, could have a catastrophic impact on your future at the company. Understanding how trust is built before entering a new job will allow you to build relationships quicker and set you up for long term success.

Embrace the Change

No matter how excited you are about the new job, it is still a big change. For some, it is a jarring change. New people. New processes or lack of processes. New commute. New computer programs. New boss. New everything. Some people underestimate how challenging it is to start a new job where you don't know anyone and have to rebuild relationships and figure out how to bring value. Starting a new job will feel like the upside-down bell curve shown on page 246.

This curve counsels that you need to give your transition some time. Starting a new job is overwhelming. Starting a new job in a new career is even crazier. And if you add in a new industry, that feeling of overwhelm can seem insurmountable. Just know that this is a major change and give yourself the gift of time to understand the new career completely before you decide whether you made the right choice.

If you are eating lunch at your desk alone, missing your old work friends, feeling unsettled in the new culture, or scrambling to understand

New Job Bell Curve

YAY! New job!
New career! I did it!

First 30 days

Oh, so this is what the
job is about... I'm not
sure about this.

90 days

People are
valuing me
and my work.
I got this!

45–75 days

First win! I'm pretty
good at this.
I get this now.

30–60 days

I should have never taken this job. I don't like this career after all.
This is the biggest mistake of my life!

the company structure, you aren't alone. I sunk to the bottom quickly when I changed careers from Viacom to Roku and then again when I went from Roku to Intuitive. But I also knew that everyone goes through this process. When I started at Intuitive, I promised myself to give it time, and if I still didn't like my job at the year mark, I would look for a new one. It took six months to settle in, and once I did, I was really happy to be there. Here are a few things I did that may help you:

1. **Be transparent.** I had an open and frank conversation with my boss about "not feeling connected" and "not fitting in." Your boss wants you to succeed. The hiring process and onboarding is long and arduous! She immediately went out and sought feedback, helped me adjust, and checked in on me during our weeklies to see how I was doing. Similar conversations with a few key colleagues also helped, as each one described their onboarding experience which was similar to mine.

2. **Let go of the old job.** Before deciding that my old job would never be a safety net, I called a leader there whom I supported and told him I wasn't sure this new role and new company was the right place for me. It was one of those "reach out and help me" calls. He was frustrated that I was in this position since he didn't want me to depart my old job in the first place. After that call, I realized I couldn't go back. I had to move forward.

3. **Look at the job through your values.** I thought about the positive aspects of my job in relation to my values. The exceptional leadership was like nothing I had ever experienced. My boss was open, communicative, and supportive. And the employees really lived the company's values of "Patient first." By focusing on the areas that aligned with my values, I was able to look at the new job hardships as the natural challenges of change and I knew in the end I would be okay. And I was. And you will be, too!

New jobs are exciting, although the transition can be rough. But you have come this far; you transitioned careers or found the perfect role. Now it is time to own it and give it everything you have to be successful. I believe in you.

Chapter 17 Summary

1. **Listen.** Speak less and listen more. Try to listen at a Level 2 or Level 3 to gain an understanding of the business, culture, and your role.

2. **Ask Questions.** Be curious. Frame thoughts, ideas, and solutions in the form of a question and you can't go wrong.

3. **Understand Expectations of the Role.** Gain an understanding of how to bring value of the role, which may be different than how you have brought value in the past.

4. **Build Relationships.** Build trust through conversation, curiosity, and understanding.

5. **Embrace the Change.** The first 90 days will be full of emotional ups and downs. Be open to discussing with your boss or a trusted colleague to get feedback on how to adjust more quickly.

Notes

Introduction

1. Co-Active Coaching Toolkit Values Clarification Exercise
   https://learn.coactive.com/hubfs/2019%20Toolkit/Co-Active
   -Coaching-Toolkit-VALUES-CLARIFICATION-EXERCISE.pdf

Chapter 1

1. David Merrill and Roger Reid. 1999. *Personal Styles and Effective Performance*. New York: CRC Press.

2. Jessica Pryce-Jones. 2010. *Happiness at Work: Maximizing Your Psychological Capital for Success*. Malden, MA: Wiley-Blackwell.

Chapter 2

1. Co-Active Coaching Toolkit Values Clarification Exercise:
   https://learn.coactive.com/hubfs/2019%20Toolkit/Co-Active-
   Coaching-Toolkit-VALUES-CLARIFICATION-EXERCISE.pdf.

2. Values cards can be found online at Amazon.com by searching "values cards" or at www.easykickstart.com.

3. Netflix documentary. 2019. *Inside Bill's Brain: Decoding Bill Gates*.

Chapter 3

1. Bruce Tulgan. 2015. Bridging the Soft Skills Gap: How to Teach the Missing Basics to Today's Young Talent. Hoboken, NJ: Jossey-Bass.

2. Megan Schaltegger. 2019. "Cadbury Is Hiring a Chocolate Taster and the Only Qualification Is 'A Passion for Confectionary.'" https://www.delish.com/food-news/a26553125/cadbury-hiring -taste-testers.

3. Orietta Gianjorio as told to Kelsey Kloss. 2021 "5 Secrets about Being a Professional Chocolate Taster." https://www.rd.com/food /fun/professional-chocolate-tasters.

Chapter 4

1. Katy Hopkins, Farran Powell, and Emma Kerr. 2020. "16 Tuition-Free Colleges." https://www.usnews.com/education/best-colleges/paying-for-college/articles/2012/06/12/save-money-by-attending-tuition-free-colleges.
2. Zack Friedman. 2019. "Here Are the Top 7 Websites for Free Online Education." https://www.forbes.com/sites/zackfriedman/2019/05/29/free-online-education/?sh=3b81f10f342b.

Chapter 6

1. Ladders, Inc. 2018. "Ladders Updates Popular Recruiter Eye-Tracking Study with New Key Insights on How Job Seekers Can Improve Their Resumes." https://www.prnewswire.com/news-releases/ladders-updates-popular-recruiter-eye-tracking-study-with-new-key-insights-on-how-job-seekers-can-improve-their-resumes-300744217.html.
2. Christina Zdanowicz and Amir Vera. 2018. "A Homeless Man Handing Out Resumes in Silicon Valley Gets More Than 200 Offers." https://www.cnn.com/2018/07/30/us/homeless-man-hands-out-resumes-trnd/index.html; https://abc7.com/society/homeless-grad-lands-job-after-handing-out-resumes-on-ca-street/4031443/.
3. Laura Italiano. 2018. "Homeless Man Hands Out Resumes, Gets Hundres of Job Offers." https://nypost.com/2018/07/28/homeless-man-hands-out-resumes-gets-hundreds-of-job-offers/; David Casarez. 2018. https://twitter.com/DavidCasarez17?ref_src=twsrc%5Etfw%7Ctwcamp%5Etweetembed%7Ctwterm%5E1032013770724237312&ref_url=https%3A%2F%2Fabc7.com%2Fsociety%2Fhomeless-grad-lands-job-after-handing-out-resumes-on-ca-street%2F4031443%2F.

Chapter 10

1. Example for illustration purposes only.
2. Nicole LaPorte. 2017. "The Reality Behind Up in the Air." https://www.thedailybeast.com/the-reality-behind-up-in-the-air.

3. Eric Cheung. 2019. "A Woman Lied on Her Resume to land a $185,000-a-year Job. Now She's Going to Jail." https://edition.cnn.com/2019/12/04/australia/australia-woman-jailed-fake-resume-intl-hnk-scli/index.html

4. https://www.nytimes.com/2006/02/21/business/radioshack-chief-resigns-after-lying.html

5. https://www.washingtonpost.com/local/public-safety/fox-news-analyst-still-wont-admit-he-was-not-in-cia/2016/07/14/eb61b5e4-478e-11e6-bdb9-701687974517_story.html

6. http://stclairmo.us

Chapter 12

1. Jeff Haden. 2017. "8 of 10 Self-Made Millionaires Were Not 'A' Students." https://www.inc.com/jeff-haden/8-of-10-self-made-millionaires-were-not-a-students-instead-they-share-this-trait.html; John Haltiwanger. 2015. "Why C Students Usually End Up Being the Most Successful in Life." https://www.elitedaily.com/money/c-students-are-successful-in-life/1039028.

Chapter 13

1. https://www.merriam-webster.com/dictionary/culture

2. Netflix. https://jobs.netflix.com/culture.

3. Sissi Cao. 2018. "Jeff Bezos and Dwight Schrute Both Hate Power-Point." https://observer.com/2018/04/why-jeff-bezos-doesnt-allow-powerpoint-at-amazon-meetings/.

4. Amazon Bound. "The Essential Package." https://amazonbound.today/p/amazon-interview-course?gclid=EAIaIQobChMIyZeS34nC5QIVj8VkCh3O2AatEAMYASAAEgLNDvD_BwE.

5. Amy Cuddy. 2015. *Presence: Bringing Your Boldest Self To Your Biggest Challenges.* New York: Little, Brown.

Chapter 15

1. Linda Babcock and Sara Laschever. 2008. *Ask for It.* New York: Bantam Dell.

2. Roger Fisher, William Urfa, and Bruce Patton. 2011. *Getting to Yes*, 3rd ed. New York: Penguin.

3. Dave Kansas. 2005. *The Wall Street Journal: Complete Money and Investing Guidebook.* New York: Three Rivers Press.

4. Randy Thurman. 2018. *More Than a Millionaire.* Oklahoma City, OK: Master Key Publications.

Chapter 17

1. Co-Active Training Institute. 2018. "Listening." https://coactive.com /blog/listening/.

2. Dennis Reina and Michelle Reina. 2006. *Trust & Betrayal in the Workplace: Building Effective Relationships in Your Organization.* San Francisco: Berrett-Koehler.

About the Author

 Marlo Lyons has spent more than 20 years inspiring, motivating, and empowering people to excel in their careers and businesses. Marlo has also successfully transferred her skills to change careers multiple times, from TV news reporter for more than a decade to entertainment lawyer, to HR Business Partner in both entertainment and the medical technology industries, to executive/career coach. Marlo started her career in Medford, Oregon, as an associate producer of medical stories for the local ABC TV affiliate. From there she became a reporter in five cities, culminating in a consumer investigative role for the CBS affiliate in Oklahoma City. After attending Oklahoma City University Law School at night, she set her sights on Los Angeles and became an entertainment lawyer at NBC and then Viacom, leading production risk management and diligence for reality shows. After more than a decade, she transformed again, obtaining her certifications in HR and coaching. She currently uses her coaching skills as a strategic HR business partner at Intuitive Surgical, where she works with senior leaders. She is also a strategic career coach for professionals worldwide. Combining her HR, career coaching, and leadership expertise with her own personal career transitions has provided her great insight into how to provide each job seeker a strategic pathway forward, whether that path means obtaining a new job at the right company, transitioning to a new career, recovering from a termination, or re-entering the workforce after a long absence.

Index